# THE RESTLESS CHURCH

# CONTENTS

## INTRODUCTION

## SECTION 1
## DECONSTRUCTION

1. We Are Too Milky
2. We Use Church For Evangelism
3. We No Longer Disciple
4. We Have Become Too Comfortable
5. We Are Active But Not Productive
6. We Have Made Our World Too Small
7. We Have Allowed The World To Become Cynical
8. We Lack The Spirit's Power
9. We Don't Get Answers In Church
10. We Love Our Traditions Too Much
11. The Story So Far
12. We Have Lost Our Men

## SECTION 2
## RECONSTRUCTION

13. What Did The Early Church Actually Look Like?
14. We Need Words & Deeds
15. The Challenge

# Introduction

I was reading a blog recently from a woman called Jennifer Taylor. It went like this:

**I have a confession to make.**

I'm tired of going to church.

After 34 years of weekly attendance, I'm bored. Bored with long sermons and the two uptempo/one slow song liturgy of our mega-church worship. I'm bored with gymnatoriums and rambling communion meditations and the tasteless cardboard bread pellets that follow. I'm bored with announcement times for ladies luncheons and small groups and choir sign-ups. I'm bored with the same clichéd phrases in the same spoken prayers offered at the same routine times.

**I'm bored.**

I know all the reasons to attend church services. But honestly, most Sunday afternoons at noon I think about other ways I could have spent the morning. Reading the New York Times with a pot of coffee, or hiking through the woods, or enjoying restorative sleep, or putzing around my kitchen trying a new recipe - these all seem more fun, productive, and restful than spending an hour at church.

It's not about being entertained. As Brett McCracken wrote in his great Wall Street Journal article last week, 70% of adults between 18-22 aren't leaving church because it's not "cool" enough. Brett wrote:

"As a twentysomething, I can say with confidence that when it comes to church, we don't want cool as much as we want "real"", he writes. "If we are interested in Christianity in any serious way, it is not because it is easy or trendy or popular. It's because Jesus himself is appealing and what he says rings true."

So I'm not looking for a slicker sermon series or faux-hawked worship leader or designer coffee in the back lobby. And...I'm not...rejecting the church universal or leaving the faith. I'm not even having a crisis of faith.

I'm just bored.

Because I believe you have to make a commitment to one local church and invest in community with those believers long-term, I'm not going to start shopping for a new church. Besides, all those churches would also have long sermons and rambling prayers and worship leaders in skinny jeans. That's the problem.

I also believe the writer of Hebrews was wise when he cautioned, "Let us not give up meeting together, as some are in the habit of doing, but let us encourage one another." I just don't find weekly church attendance that encouraging anymore. In addition to its predictability, I have plenty of friends who also attend church each weekend and then get drunk, live with their boyfriends, or swear the air blue. In the south, church attendance is traditional. It is a habit, and one that doesn't, in itself, produce life change.

So I'm sincerely unsure of the solution. Church, with two songs/greeting/awkward handshakes/one song/communion/offering/sermon/two songs/dismissal, is *how our culture does Christianity. And I'm ready for something else.*

http://writeaboutnowjt.wordpress.com/2010/08/17/church-fatigue/

What she is describing is church fatigue. A boredom with the status quo. A restlessness with the predictability; the traditions; the liturgical routines; the lack of righteousness and real change in those who attend services; the way the church is overly concerned with image rather than authenticity. She is describing a craving for something more dynamic, more real and more effective.

We can try to dismiss her as a whiney victim of consumerist culture and we can whip out the old line about no church being perfect and tell her to plough on regardless, but the truth is she is representing the voice of a growing minority. There's a growing feeling that something is missing from our church experience. The church as a whole is getting restless.

The problem is that even though many are restless, they just don't know what else they can do! A pastor replied to Jennifer Taylor's blog saying:

*"Jennifer, I know and feel exactly what you're talking about. (Here's the usual disclaimer) I'm not a 30-something. I'm a 50-something.*

*Now here's the UNusual disclaimer. I'm the senior-minister-preacher-worship-minister for our congregation. I'm the guy who is in charge of making it all happen each week. And much of the time, I MYSELF am bored senseless with what we do. I have a masters degree in worship ministry, from a program full of very hip California-types, who are all about "engaging worship" and such. And yet I experienced the same boredom in so many places where I've visited, from coast to coast.*

*Every week is a struggle to make things more interesting, more engaging, more fulfilling - but just about each week, I fall into the same formula, the same songs, the same lineup and order and blah blah blah. Some weeks, it works. Some weeks, it doesn't."*

The way that we do church has been set in stone for so long now that if 'church' doesn't mean an 11am service by the usual formula, we don't know what it *does* mean! If we don't follow the age-old template, we wouldn't know what else we're supposed to do. We wouldn't know what it was supposed to look like. And so, pastors like this one, working within the strict confines of this template, believing the template to be sacred and immovable, or at least not being able to visualise any alternative, simply try to move things around a bit. They change running orders, jazz things up with more multimedia or introduce some new songs into the worship time. Since they can't change the template they simply try to fight with it to get it to work so that it becomes more engaging and more fulfilling.

Yet the church remains restless and many are leaving.

Jennifer Taylor quoted Brett McCracken in her blog as saying that 70% of young adults between 18-22 are turning their back on church. I haven't been able to verify those shocking figures but all independent research seems to support the theory that the Western institutional church is in decline. Olson says that less than 20% of Americans now regularly attend church services. Olson also predicts that if current trends continue, church attendance in 2050 will be half of what it was in 1990. Prominent researcher Thom Rainer suggests that only 6% of institutional churches in the US are growing at a faster rate than their community's population growth. In other words, the formal church as a whole is losing ground in the West. People are simply walking away from it.

When the church is haemorrhaging attendees and those that remain are restless, we can only conclude that something has gone terribly wrong. But does that mean that all hope lost? Is the church destined to continue falling irreversibly into decline? These surface statistics would suggest so but I personally do think there is cause for great hope in all of this. In fact, I believe the Holy Spirit is at work.

You see, boredom with the status quo is causing the Restless Church to examine itself in ways we possibly haven't seen since the Reformation. And this is a good thing. It's causing us to question the old formulas and the traditional templates. We're beginning to ask, *"what if church doesn't have to be 11am, Sunday morning, two songs, greeting, awkward handshakes, one song, communion, offering, sermon, two songs, dismissal? What if that formula is not sacred after all?"*

The restlessness is causing us to look to the Bible for answers. Neil Cole said, *"Many people are longing for a greater cause. They are no longer content with 'church as usual.' They read of the church in the New Testament, and their curiosity is piqued. The New Testament accounts are far removed from their experience every week. They hear contemporary stories of the church expanding rapidly in parts of China and India, and their hearts soar."*

Thirst is uncomfortable but it's the discomfort that causes us to go looking for water. Hunger is uncomfortable but it's the discomfort that causes us to go looking for food. Restlessness with church is uncomfortable but it's the discomfort that is causing us to go looking for New Testament Christianity. People are starting to come to the Bible with new questions. They're starting to ask why our church experience is so far removed from that of the New Testament. We realise that there's something very different happening in the Book of Acts to anything we've ever known or seen with our own eyes and it's starting to bother us. Something which seems so thrilling, real, authentic and powerful in the pages of the Bible seems to have been rendered so dull, fake, hypocritical and weak by our contemporary formulas. It's the restlessness that is actually driving the change.

You see, all those negative statistics about the decline of the institutional church are hiding something important: Many people who are walking away are not doing so as "back-sliders" or because of a crisis of faith - quite the opposite - they're walking away because they're looking for something *more* meaningful. *More* authentic. They're looking for *more* of Jesus; not less. Not finding him in stale, routine services, they've simply gone looking for him outside of the four walls of the institutional church.

Ed Stetzer, director of the Center For Missional Research at the North American Mission Board has discovered that a growing number of people are finding Christian discipleship and community in places other than their local church buildings. His study found that an astonishing 24.5% of such Americans now say their primary form of spiritual nourishment is meeting with a small group of 20 or less people every week. Stetzer says, "About 6 million people meet weekly with a small group and never or rarely go to church services. There is a significant movement happening." Prior to the release of this book I questioned Fuel Project subscribers through the Facebook page about how often they attend formal church services and without prompting, many of them confirmed that they felt they had to *leave* church services to find Jesus. They now meet informally in small groups and have no desire to go back to the old routine. I talked with others and was surprised at how often this sentiment arose.

Not only is the template not working for us, it's not working for the world either. People look at church now with extreme cynicism and suspicion. Relevant Magazine polled a range of non-Christians between the ages of 16-29 and discovered that between 70-91% of them thought the church could *primarily* be defined as judgmental, hypocritical, old-fashioned, too political, out of touch with reality and insensitive to others. These were the traits they *most* associated with Christianity.

What went wrong? How did a church with a message so compelling that it changed the world get so off-track? This book is designed to answer that question. And it's designed to do it in a very specific way. Firstly we're going to spend some time *deconstructing* the image of church we currently have. Then we're then going to spend some time *reconstructing* it according to the New Testament example. In other words, we need to dismantle what *is*, before we can rebuild what *should be*. At the end of all this, we're looking for a return to the Christian faith that we see demonstrated in the New Testament.

Please note, as we go through the deconstruction process we're going to be making a lot of generalisations. Generalisations are just that - general. That is, they are not specific to every congregation in every community around the world. If something in the pages ahead doesn't apply to your particular congregation then ignore it and move to the next stage. The most important thing, what we're aiming for above all else, is to create a clean slate in our minds, devoid of all the old myths and man-made traditions that currently plague us, so that we are unhindered from building a fresh image of church in our minds. An image purely inspired by the Word of God.

I believe the Holy Spirit is already driving this change and my hope is that this book will clarify why it has to happen.

# Section 1
# Deconstruction

# Chapter 1
# We're Too Milky

*"There is today no lack of Bible teachers to set forth correctly the principles of the doctrine of Christ, but too many of these seem satisfied to teach the fundamentals of the faith year after year, strangely unaware that there is in their ministry no manifest Presence, nor anything unusual in their personal lives. They minister constantly to believers who feel within their breast a longing which their teaching simply does not satisfy."* - A.W. Tozer

---

We have a widely used phrase in English, "preaching to the choir". The phrase originated in American churches in the 1970s but actually grew out of a phrase that was in circulation from the 1860s, "preaching to the converted". The idea being expressed here is that it is pointless trying to make believers out of people who already believe, or convince people who are already convinced. It's a waste of time and energy. The secular equivalent of the phrase would be, "kicking at an open door". There's no point in putting such time and effort into opening the door - it's already open. There's no point in preaching up a storm to convert Christians - they're already converted.

How does a Christian become 'converted'? Simply by responding to a message known as the Gospel. The Gospel explains that everyone has sinned and that those sins have separated us from God. It tells us that although our just punishment is death, God loved us so much that He sent his one and only begotten Son, Jesus Christ, into the world to take that punishment for our sins upon Himself and because of His death and resurrection, He has created a way for us to be reconciled with God. If we repent of our sins and put our faith in Him, He will grant us eternal life.

This Gospel is the absolute foundational doctrine of the Christian faith and our response to it defines whether we are a Christian or not. It's the message we give to unbelievers in an attempt to convince them of their need of a Saviour. In other words it is square one. The starting point. Jesus said, *"I tell you the truth, those who listen to my message and believe in God who sent me have eternal life..." (John 5:24)* We have eternal life if we respond to the Gospel in the right way.

So what would we conclude if we went to a church full of mature Christians who had been saved for 5, 10, 15 or 50 years and discovered that the pastor was preaching this same foundational Gospel message to them week-in, week-out? Surely we would conclude that the pastor was kicking at an open door? That he was wasting his time and energy? *"Why is he trying to convince people who are already convinced?"* we would think. *"Why is he trying to make believers out of people who already believe?"*

Yet in my experience, this is what is happening in many church services every Sunday morning. A feeling has grown amongst pastors...and some church attendees...that if the message of "Jesus Christ and Him crucified" isn't preached from the platform on a Sunday morning, then it's not a valid, satisfactory, nor "Biblical" sermon.

And so a peculiar scenario has developed whereby many Christians go to church to hear a message they already know and accept, from a pastor who already knows they know it, and knows they accept it. And what is exceptionally strange in some circles, is that some of these Christians will get disgruntled if they *don't* hear this information that they already know and accept! In some cases then, church has merely become an exercise in perfecting the art of "preaching to the choir". A pointless ritual where a lot of time and energy is wasted weekly telling people things they already know. It sounds controversial but for most Christians, hearing another Gospel message is actually the last thing they need.

In fact, the Bible specifically warns against never moving beyond square one like this. The writer to the Hebrews says,

*"You have been believers so long now that you ought to be teaching others. Instead, you need someone to teach you again the basic things about God's word. You are like babies who need milk and cannot eat solid food. For someone who lives on milk is still an infant and doesn't know how to do what is right. Solid food is for those who are mature, who through training have the skill to recognize the difference between right and wrong."* - Hebrews 5:12-14

What is this milk that the Hebrews writer is talking about? What is this fundamental teaching they have never moved beyond? The next chapter goes on:

*"So let us stop going over the basic teachings about Christ again and again. Let us go on instead and become mature in our understanding. Surely we don't need to start again with the fundamental importance of repenting from evil deeds and placing our faith in God. You don't need further instruction*

*about baptisms, the laying on of hands, the resurrection of the dead, and eternal judgment. And so, God willing, we will move forward to further understanding."* - Hebrews 6:1-3

"Milk" is the Gospel message! Milk is why we should repent of 'evil deeds' and 'place our faith in God' to avoid 'eternal judgement'. The writer to the Hebrews is saying, "why are you going over these basic things time and time again? Why aren't you progressing?"

Our sinful nature and the need for repentance and faith in Jesus for everlasting life...these are things that Christians already know. We already know what Jesus achieved on the cross, we understand it, we've heard it explained literally hundreds of times. What is more, we have accepted it, put our faith in Christ and we don't need any more convincing. We are now the choir. We are the converted. The Gospel message is completely foundational. It's the starting point. Square one. It is milk for non-believers and 'infant' Christians. But there's so much more to explore and discover about this world through the lens of that Gospel message. There is so much solid food to get into as we grow and mature. There is so much more building we need to do on top of those foundations. If we simply keep going over and over the basics again and again, we will never progress.

Paul wrote to the Corinthians using this same metaphor saying, *"Dear brothers and sisters, when I was with you I couldn't talk to you as I would to spiritual people. I had to talk as though you belonged to this world or as though you were infants in the Christian life. I had to feed you with milk, not with solid food, because you weren't ready for anything stronger. And you still aren't ready, for you are still controlled by your sinful nature..."* - 1 Corinthians 3:1-3

If a parent feeds a newborn baby with milk, the child will initially grow because it contains all the nutrients the baby's body needs. In fact, at that stage in the baby's development, milk is *exactly* what's required. The infant's stomach isn't yet ready to cope with solid food. However, there comes a stage in the child's life when milk alone no longer has what it takes to fuel their development and solid food is required. If the parent doesn't make this transition to solids at the right time, the child will become malnourished and their growth will be stunted.

In this passage to the Corinthians, Paul is saying there is basic, milky teaching which is beneficial for non-Christians and baby Christians - that teaching is *exactly* what is required at that early stage in our lives - but if we want to really mature, we must eventually move onto stronger, solid food. If we don't, we become spiritually malnourished and our growth is compromised.

Let me illustrate using another example.

When a child first starts school they will learn that 1+1 = 2. That's probably the most basic and foundational mathematical sum there is. Now to a five year old child, 1+1 is actually a tough concept to grasp. At that early stage in their development, the child needs to be switched on and engaged to get an understanding of what this arithmetic thing is all about.

But imagine if the years rolled by and every week the teacher taught the same thing. Imagine if the child is now twelve years old and is still being taught that 1+1 = 2. Imagine the child has never been introduced to more complex addition, subtraction, division, multiplication, fractions, percentages or algebra. In this case their growth would be stunted. They would not have matured. Though they are now entering their teenage years they would still only have the understanding of a five year old. What is more, the child would now be bored, restless, disengaged, seeing no benefit or purpose in coming to class anymore and maybe even looking for answers from other sources.

Just as your school teachers constantly pushed back your horizons and led you into deeper understanding at school, building on what you already knew year-on-year, we should be looking for similar progression in our spiritual lives. And if we don't get that sense of progression and are constantly being fed the spiritual version of 1+1, we will become bored, restless, disengaged, will cease to see the benefit or purpose in coming to church anymore, and will start looking for answers from other sources.

## Restless, Bored & Disengaged

I saw a pastor write this on Facebook recently, *"The difference in spiritual hunger between Chinese students at [church] and regular Brits, is startling. As I preached a simple Gospel on Sunday, the Chinese were perched on the edge of their seats, and full of questions at the end, engaging with a bible study on the sermon over lunch. While it's difficult to read body language when you're in full flow, most others seemed to be stifling yawns. That is a picture of world Christianity at the moment. The East is ablaze, the west is asleep, with exactly the same Gospel. Still, who cares...so long as we have a merry christmas..."*

These words are clearly filled with frustration and I can see why. It must be extremely frustrating to preach passionately week-in and week-out and find that it doesn't seem to be motivating the church or rousing any emotion. To preach your heart out but find that everyone is just as apathetic going out as coming in. I guess the pastor may look for numerous solutions or reasons as to why this should be the case. Perhaps he should re-double his efforts and preach it twice as hard in the hope that it will re-evoke the passion that all Christians first feel when they meet Jesus. Perhaps, as this pastor seems to feel, it's a cultural thing or some judgement from God to harden the hearts of the people in a particular part of the world.

I propose that the reason is far more obvious.

It's simply that the basic Gospel message to mature converts is like a teacher trying to teach college students what 1+1 is. We know it. We get it. We understand it. We accept it. There's no need to kick at an open door. There's no need to try to convert the converted and make believers out of those who already believe. We're in. We've already signed up. But what comes next?

Imagine a school teacher getting exasperated with 18 year old university students saying, "why are you not grasping 1+1? Why are you not excited about it? Why are you not perched on the edge of your seats and taking notes like the five year old kids are?" The students may well reply, "we grasped it a long time ago and we *were* excited about it when we were their age...but what now? Where do we go from here? We've long been ready to be challenged with more...."

These are the questions many Christians are asking themselves. We get the Gospel message. Really. But what comes next? Is this it? Are we just going to come to a church service every Sunday to hear variations of this same message for the rest of our lives? Is that what Christianity is? Sitting in services trying to coerce ourselves into feeling the same level of excitement we had about the Gospel message as when we first believed? Is merely *feeling* excited or emotional the end goal here?

Some pastors would have you believe that.

And so many Christians who attend church services begin feel guilty about the restlessness and boredom they experience when they turn up on a Sunday morning to hear yet another Gospel message. And you can see why it's easy to feel guilty. This is, after all, the greatest message there is. This is the most glorious event in all of history. The pivotal event that created a way for us to have everlasting life! Wow. The magnitude and beauty of the Gospel message really can't be overstated. What a glorious message! And it truly is the foundation of everything we believe. And how absolutely vital it is that we get our understanding of it right before we attempt to move on to anything else. When builders build houses, the foundations are the most important part of the structure and take longest to establish. And it's the same with the Christian life. We must make sure the foundations are right. I certainly do not want to diminish the importance or sheer majesty of the Gospel. But at the same time, we must not lose sight of the fact that foundations are simply that - foundational. Once you have grasped it and accepted it, there is simply no need to go over it again and again and again. Like the Hebrews writer says, that's actually detrimental to your growth. At some point you must move forward and build on those strong foundations. (Matt 7:24-29)

You may be one of those who is misinterpreting your own restlessness in church thinking, "I'm bored with this. And since the problem plainly can't be with the message, the problem must be with me. My heart must have grown cold. This isn't moving me like it once did. I must be drifting or backsliding. I'm not perched on the edge of my seat. I don't *feel* the same level of excitement as when I first believed." Not necessarily. If you were to listen to the same song every day you may get bored of that song but it wouldn't necessarily follow that you have become bored of music altogether. If you drink milk every day you will eventually become bored of milk, but that doesn't mean you've ceased to have any appetite at all. Similarly, if you hear the same message at church every week you may get bored of that message but it doesn't necessarily follow you have no appetite for Jesus. On the contrary, the more likely explanation is that you're ready for something deeper and more substantial. You're ready to move from nursery rhymes to concertos. You're ready to move from milk to meat. It's not necessarily cause for concern if you don't *feel* the same heights of emotion as you once did every time you hear the same gospel message.

## Feelings

Listen to this observation on feelings by CS Lewis: *"Being in love is a good thing, but it is not the best thing. There are many things below it, but there are also many things above it. You cannot make it the basis of a whole life. It is a noble feeling, but it is still a feeling. Now no feeling can be relied on to last in its full intensity, or even to last at all. Knowledge can last, principles can last, habits can last; but feelings come and go. And in fact, whatever people say, the state called "being in love" usually does not last. If the old fairy-tale ending "They lived happily ever after" is taken to mean "They felt for the next fifty years exactly as they felt the day before they were married," then it says what probably never was or ever could be true, and would be highly undesirable if it were. Who could bear to live in that excitement for even five years? What would become of your work, your appetite, your sleep, your friendships? But, of course, ceasing to be "in love" need not mean ceasing to love. Love in this second sense — love as distinct from "being in love" is not merely a feeling. It is a deep unity, maintained by the will and deliberately strengthened by habit; reinforced by (in Christian marriages) the grace which both parents ask, and receive, from God...They can retain this love even when each would easily, if they allowed themselves, be "in love" with someone else. "Being in love" first moved them to promise fidelity: this quieter love enables them to keep the promise. It is on this love that the engine of marriage is run: being in love was the explosion that started it." (Mere Christianity)*

CS Lewis is describing a relationship between a man and a woman but a similar thing happens in our spiritual lives - in our 'marriage' with Christ, if you will. When we first meet Jesus we experience an explosion of excitement similar to that feeling of being in love and that's the ignition spark that starts our relationship. But by-and-by that initial thrill of euphoria will give way to a quieter and more enduring love. That second type of love for Christ is the engine on which our relationship with Him is run. It is a love that is maintained by the will and deliberately strengthened by habit. It is reinforced in our daily walk with Him, our prayer times, Bible study, our acts of kindness and generosity for others and our God-glorifying ministries. These are things that can be sustained over the course of a lifetime and as we are intentional about them our relationship with Him will deepen.

The feelings of euphoria will come and go throughout your life. I still often get them when I hear certain songs or see a beautiful landscape or sunset. They're great when they arrive. But like all feelings, they can never be relied upon to remain in their full intensity and will leave as quickly as they came. And this is ok. Really. Because feelings are *not* the thing on which your relationship with God is run. In the same way that feelings are not the thing on which a marriage are run. Feelings are volatile but true love is an act of the will. If you make it the goal of your Christian life to always just *feel* the same level of excitement you had when you first met Jesus by listening to the same Gospel message over and over again, and then judge your spiritual condition on those feelings, you will only experience frustration, guilt and anguish. Furthermore, it's missing the point. Feeling euphoric is not the end-goal of Christianity.

The frustrated pastor observed on his Facebook post that there was a striking difference between British people and Chinese people during his Gospel sermon. Philip Yancey talked about this difference in an interview for the Christian Post saying, *"when I go around the world I kind of divide the church up into three stages: the honeymoon, the divorce stage, and the 25-year marriage stage. So you go to Europe and they're pretty much in the divorce stage. Now there's still the shell of churches but tourists, not worshippers. You go to a place like Brazil, where we were, or the Philippines, China and you see the church in the honeymoon stage – It's all new, they're excited, it's thrilling, it sounds like good news."*

The Gospel message is simply new to the Chinese. They haven't heard it before. They're spiritual infants who need this milk. They're in the first flush of love and they're getting the same explosion of excitement that we had when we first heard the Gospel. It rightly thrills them. But if their pastors keep giving them milk and don't move onto solid food, the Chinese culture will be where Europe is within a few generations. Bored, restless and disengaged and looking for answers from other sources. It needn't be this way. There is no fundamental reason why the church in various parts of the world should reach a 'divorce' stage with God at all. But we must look for *progression*.

Lewis continues with his thoughts on 'feelings' saying, "*It is simply no good trying to keep any thrill: that is the very worst thing you can do. Let the thrill go — let it die away — go on through that period of death into the quieter interest and happiness that follow — and you will find you are living in a world of new thrills all the time. But if you decide to make thrills your regular diet and try to prolong them artificially, they will all get weaker and weaker, and fewer and fewer, and you will be a bored, disillusioned old man for the rest of your life...It is much better fun to learn to swim than to go on endlessly (and hopelessly) trying to get back the feeling you had when you first went paddling as a small boy.*"

When we make "feeling excited about the Gospel" our end goal, we will find the initial thrill getting weaker and we will become bored and disillusioned. It's only as we progress that we will discover we are living in a world of new thrills all the time. Rather than trying to get back the feeling we had when we first went paddling, we must learn how to swim. Rather than trying to get back the feeling we had on our first date, we must learn to get married, have children, find new hobbies, have grandchildren. And rather than trying to get back to the feeling we had when we first heard the Gospel, we must progress in our spiritual walk and build on those foundations. We must learn to see that the Gospel is the beginning of the journey for us; not the end. It's only the first step. We must continually push back horizons. Dream bigger dreams. Attempt bigger things. Reach new goals. And as we do so, we will discover we are living in a world of new thrills all the time. We will rediscover that a true walk with God is far from boring; it is in fact the most exciting way to live.

All this begs the question though; why do so many pastors insist on giving us milk anyway?

## Chapter 2
## We Use Church For Evangelism

Imagine that a new school opens up in town and hundreds of children between the ages of 5 to 12 enrol. On the first day of term the children assemble together in the main hall of the school expecting to be divided into their age related classes and assigned an individual teacher. But instead, the Principal gets up on stage and explains to the children that they won't be divided into classes, there are no other teachers, and that he will be educating them all personally, all at once, in the same room.

As the Principle gazes over the room he suddenly realises he has foolishly created a problem for himself.

Because if he aims his teaching at the oldest children in the room, the twelve year olds, everyone *below* twelve years old will be left clueless. They'll become bored, confused and frustrated because they don't have the foundational knowledge in place from which to understand these more complicated things. There's no use him teaching advanced algebra when some of them don't even know 1+1 yet. He's only going to alienate the majority if he takes this route.

Now if the Principle drops down a year and aims his teaching at the eleven year olds, this is slightly more inclusive. OK, the twelve year olds won't be learning anything new by this method - they already went over this stuff last year - but at least he's now reaching two age groups with information they both understand. And he could argue, I suppose, that it will be good for the oldest ones to refresh their memories. However, the problem remains that he would still be leaving behind everyone *below* the age of eleven.

The same thing will happen if he aims at the 10, 9, 8, 7 or 6 year olds. Whichever age group he aims for, everyone below that age will be left behind. The only way he can be fully inclusive and make sure *everyone* hears something they can understand is if he aims for the lowest common denominator - the five year olds. This is the *most* inclusive strategy. If he teaches the foundational things, the five year olds will be learning something new and although the rest of the older kids already know this stuff and won't be advancing as such, they will at least understand what he's saying. He could also argue that it won't harm the older kids to go over the basics again. Everyone needs a refresher course from time-to-time.

This habit of aiming at the lowest common denominator in order to reach the widest possible audience is well-known to occur in all areas of life. In the media it has been referred to as "dumbing down". TV and radio stations do it because it brings in the highest ratings for their shows. Ultimately, it has a negative impact on society because, as the name suggests, it slows down and even reverses intellectual and social development.

But this is effectively what pastors can fall into the habit of doing on Sundays. As they get up on the platform and look out at the hundreds of faces in the congregation, there is an assumption that on any given week, amongst the many mature Christians, there will be at least two or three non-Christians or infant Christians scattered around the room who may not have heard or grasped the Gospel before. Milk is exactly what these spiritual five-year-olds need. He wants to reach them. He doesn't want to leave them baffled and put off from ever coming back. He wants the church to grow with new believers. That is, after all, why the church exists: to preach the Good News to a dying world. "And well" he thinks, "it won't harm the mature believers if they hear this again. This is the foundation of our faith after all. And it's their fault if they're not perched on the edge of their seats with wide-eyed excitement like these non-believers are."

And so church services can often become primarily concerned with evangelism - the proclamation of the Gospel to unbelievers. This is when the preaching to the converted can take place. Many is the time I've left a church service and heard a mature Christian saying, "well I didn't hear anything new today but it will have been good for any non-believers who were there." As long as the message has reached a non-believer, real or imagined, we're willing to put our own progress to the side. This is an admirable, self-sacrificial attitude...but a wholly misguided one. As the writer to the Hebrews explains, if the teaching is always milk aimed at the spiritual infants, the rest of the church is going to suffer from arrested development. We're going to end up with spiritually dull, Biblically illiterate, weak, shallow, ineffective and restless Christians. In a world that *desperately* needs the opposite.

So how do we solve this problem? How do we reach two groups with one message on a Sunday morning? How do we make sure we evangelise to the non-Christians without neglecting the progress of the mature Christians at the same time?

The answer is that we shouldn't. We've lost sight of what the church is *for*.

## WHAT IS THE CHURCH FOR?

Here's how things worked in the early church. The believers would come together, eat together, pray together, sing together, study together, and then, having been recharged, blessed and encouraged by being in the presence of one another, they would then go out into the public sphere to preach the Gospel to the world. Out in the world they would experience hatred, persecution, threats and violence for the message that they preached. Exactly like Jesus promised they would. There would be imprisonments. There would be beatings. There would even be martyrdom. But there would also be converts. Some people would come to salvation in Christ.

After these co-ordinated forays into the world, the believers would come back together to recuperate with fellow believers, eating together, praying together, singing together, studying together, exhorting one another to keep the faith and fight the good fight in spite of all the tribulation. After being recharged, blessed and encouraged by being in the one another's company once more, they would then head back out into the world for another raid into enemy territory. Fulfilling the Great Commission wherever they went. Preaching the Gospel, healing the sick, casting out demons. And the same things would happen as always. Persecution. Hatred. Riots. Revivals.

In other words, the church gatherings were just a base for Christians. A training camp. A place to be equipped and empowered for the real work of reaching and saving the lost. And then the work of evangelism was done out there, outside of the four walls, outside of their cosy fellowship, in the public arena. Evangelism was for the market place, the town square, the debating forums, the street corners. The church gatherings themselves were *not* for evangelism. Church gatherings were for believers only. A place of relative safety for them to come together with their brothers and sisters in Christ to plan, strategise, learn and build each other up between daring forays into the world.

Look through the pages of the New Testament and you'll find that all evangelism occurs in a public setting. There was a sending out culture in the church and every believer was expected to play their part. Each one would be equipped to make converts or to play some part in reaching the world. Each one had to know what they believed and why they believed it and had to be ready to make a defence of their faith at any given moment in public (1 Peter 3:15). Every one of them was a labourer for the kingdom in some way. Again, church gatherings were simply where they trained and planned for that labour.

Notice there is a kind of tidal motion to this. Come in, go out, come in, go out, come in, go out....

Today we have lost much of that going out culture. We're very good at the coming in part. We're very good at meetings, conferences and passively listening to sermons. But we have lost the concept that evangelism is our job. We have lost the idea that we are to *go*. The very thought that we should tell others about Jesus fills us with dread. How we'd get laughed at, the friends we'd lose, the anger and resentment we'd face, the questions we'd be unable to answer... it would be terrible! And often we're just too apathetic to put ourselves through all that. Fear and Apathy has chained the Western church down and rendered it insular and largely ineffective.

No, we're quite happy coming into a comfortable, cosy sanctuary to watch an entertaining show on a Sunday morning and staying there. That's enough for us. Knowing how to explain the Gospel, defend the faith, answer difficult questions about evolution, false religion, hell and whatnot, *"well that's the pastor's job. That's what we pay him for. He's the professional."* With this mindset, our evangelism efforts with friends and co-workers, if any, are often reduced to, *"hey, why don't you come to church with me this Sunday?"* Because we've lost the "go" part of our culture and are now only left with the "come" part, we no longer try to reach people where they are but instead try to reach people where we are. In other words, we try to reach them without moving out from our comfortable setting. We bring our unsaved friends along with us to the church building and then sit beside them for an hour silently hoping and praying that the pastor doesn't preach anything too deep or controversial and that he will get around to a milky Gospel message that our unbelieving friend can understand. This is better than nothing - at least we're still trying to reach them - but to be honest we're ducking our responsibilities and creating the dilemma for pastors, who are now trying to reach two groups with one message. The pastors themselves are often equally to blame for this problem. How many times have you heard your pastor wrap up his sermon with, *"Hey, next week, why don't you bring along a friend who doesn't know Jesus?"* and you just know that this is code for, *"next week will be pure milk. Don't expect to hear anything you don't already know. You'll be expected to sit it out while we try to reach your unbelieving friends."* We're getting it wrong here. We shouldn't be looking to bring people to church; we should be looking to bring church to the people.

Jesus' last command to us before his ascension was to *"**go** make disciples of all nations, baptising them in the name of the Father and the Son and the Holy Spirit. Teach these new disciples to obey all the commands I have given you. And be sure of this: I* *am with you always, even to the end of the age."* (Matt 28:19-20) This Great Commission to *go* was a command to *every* single Christian. It was a command to you and me. We are *all* called to play a proactive role. We are all called to go. Therefore, it is not the pastor's job to evangelise on a Sunday morning; it's to equip and train the body of Christ to go and evangelise throughout the week. Outside the four walls of church in the public arena.

The best thing a pastor can do then is make sure that these Christians, who are being sent out like sheep amongst wolves, are as ready as they can be to face the challenges and persecution they will inevitably experience in the public sphere. We need believers who are trained and equipped to the highest possible level. We need Christians who are as spiritually strong and knowledgeable as they possibly can be. At the very peak of their potential. Proficient with their God-given gifts. To that end we need to make sure there is high quality, deep, progressive teaching in the church so that people are constantly maturing.

Let's lay this on the line. The spread of the Gospel is the most important mission of the church. To save the lost is the reason the church exists. As CS Lewis wrote, *"The church exists for nothing else but to draw men into Christ, to make them little Christs. If they are not doing that, all the cathedrals, clergy, missions, sermons, even the Bible itself, are simply a waste of time. God became Man for no other purpose."* We're going to have lots of time in the next life, once this world has faded away, to relax and live in comfort but that's not our calling in this life. In this life we have work to do. In order to fulfil the Great Commission we simply must go to where the lost are. Evangelism is not an insular, cosy or comfortable activity.

If you ask the average Christian how many people they talked to about Jesus last week, the most common answer will be "zero". We're largely ignoring the Great Commission because our comfort has made us apathetic and we're too afraid of the backlash we'd receive. Instead we're trying to lure people into our buildings so we can lay all the responsibility on professional clergy who are then left with a dilemma of trying to reach two audiences from the platform on a Sunday morning. Often that leads them to preach "milk" and this holds back the overall training of the church. But what's perhaps even more worrying is that the average Christian wouldn't know where to begin making disciples of others. Because very few of us have actually been truly discipled ourselves.

## Chapter 3
## We No Longer Disciple

Francis Chan said something very interesting.

"We had these communist revolutions in China and in Russia. In both revolutions they were trying to kill the church. The whole point was destroying the church.

Now in Russia, everything was built around cathedrals and these priests. Everything was centred around these buildings and these teachers. The moment the government took away these teachers and the church assets, the people didn't know where to turn. They didn't know how to grow. They didn't know how to disciple. And so the church basically died.

In China the same thing happened. Under Mao Tse Tung, they got rid of all the buildings. But there was something different about the church in China. See, before all that happened, they had empowered the ordinary Christians. And the ordinary Christians knew how to lead others to the Lord. The every-day church attendee knew how to teach others how to grow in their faith. So when [the Communist Party] took away the leaders, and they took away the buildings...the church was fine! The people were fine. In fact, under Mao Tse Tung, the church, the persecuted church, grew from 2 million to an estimated 80 million in underground gatherings.

*Why? Because the people understood how to minister to other people. They knew how to teach other people.*

*I want you to look at your life and think, 'which camp would I fall into? Would I be one of those who would be lost and wondering, 'what do I do now? The building's gone, the leadership's gone...' Or would you just think, 'we don't really need a building, and I know the Word of God, and I know how to lead other people...'"*

Are we "Russia" or "China"? I believe the answer is so clear. You see, what we have done is divided ourselves into professional clergy and laity. Under this system the clergy are basically expected to do all the work and the laity are expected to turn up and enjoy the show. Occasionally, we may bring an unbeliever along with us but the actual work of evangelising and teaching and discipling is something we regard as the clergy's job. For that reason it's been said that churches today are like a football game. The twenty-two players on the field are in dire need of a rest and the 100,000 spectators in the stands are in dire need of some exercise! We have, in all honesty, become lazy. We've created a church culture where we pay pastors to do the ministry and the rest of us show up, go through the motions, put some money in the plate, and leave feeling inspired, fed, excited or challenged. If we *feel* any of those things then we think that's all there is to it. We did the "come in" part so it's job done. Good service. Pat on the back for the pastor. The only "going out" we intend to do now is for lunch. We have moved so far away from Jesus' command to go make disciples for ourselves that many Christians don't have a frame of reference for what that actually looks like. If there wasn't a building to invite people to and we didn't have the clergy doing it for us, we'd be lost! We wouldn't know how to lead others to

Christ. We wouldn't know how to disciple people for ourselves. Many of us wouldn't even know the Word of God because the only time we ever expose ourselves to it is when the pastor's teaching it on a Sunday morning. We have become so passive that we have developed a complete dependency on organisational structures, which has, in turn, made us individually weak and spiritually dull.

On January 3, 2012, Relevant Magazine posted an article on why so many young Christians are leaving the church in America. An unnamed pastor left this comment: *"The church needs to more intentionally blur the lines between clergy and laity, removing the "come and watch" mentality that so many sitting in pews week-in and week-out are actually experiencing. Apart from a relationship, both with Christ and with His Body, nobody will stick with "church". Truthfully, it's not that great a show. As a pastor, we have to lead out in this. Much of the problem is our fault. We have created the "Sunday Show" environment in an effort to "reach" as many as we can. And while that is a worthwhile desire, to reach as many as possible, we have missed the trees for the forest. We have equated attendance with commitment. We have substituted discipleship with classes. A thriving "Small Group Network" will help ease the exodus, but it will not fix the problem. Somewhere, somehow we have to re-engage the principles of authentic community within our churches. The way we "do" church has to change. Otherwise we will be having these same discussions in another 20 years."*

I love what this guy is saying. We must reverse the idea that church is a show presented by a professional organisation which we are to come and watch passively on a Sunday morning. We must remove this feeling of dependency on a hierarchy of professional clergy and the buildings they inhabit. As the end-times approach and the spirit of Anti-Christ rises, we may not have those things much longer anyway. The time is coming when Christianity will be outlawed, either by our own governments, or by the future one world government, and persecution will be certain for those who continue in the faith. Public gatherings will simply not be possible. Therefore, if we retain a "Russian" dependency on buildings and professional clergy, when those things are taken away, we will be decimated. We must instead move towards a persecution-proof "Chinese" model where we are individually empowered to lead and disciple. I believe the Holy Spirit is causing a restlessness with the current "Russian" system and compelling us towards a "Chinese" system (which is, incidentally, the New Testament system) because we need to be prepared for the dark days of tribulation which lie ahead.

We must understand that professional clergy, buildings and all the trappings that we currently associate with the institutional church, are in fact, not the church. Very simply, you are the church. We are the church. The church is the organic body of Christ. In order to make that body strong, we must empower and equip every Christian to grow, serve, teach and become leaders of their own. And in order to do all this, we must return to true discipleship. Because as the pastor above wrote, in most churches today, we have substituted true discipleship with mere education.

## We Educate Rather Than Disciple

We tend to think of discipleship as mere education because that's all we've ever known, but true discipleship is actually far more extensive. While education is, or can be, passive - listening to sermons, sitting in classes, lectures or seminars - true discipleship crucially adds practical application into the mix. It follows the tidal motion that I mentioned earlier. Jesus drew his disciples around him to teach and then he sent them out to apply the message. He drew them back in to teach something new and then he sent them out to apply again. This is the rhythm of discipleship and it became the rhythm of the early church. Hear, apply, hear, apply, hear, apply, hear, apply. Hearing of course, is the easy bit. Actually going out to apply what you're learning is the hard bit. But James exhorts us saying, *"But don't just listen to God's word. You must do what it says. Otherwise, you are only fooling yourselves."* (James 1:22) Jesus himself said, *"why do you keep calling me 'Lord, Lord!' when you don't do what I say?"* (Luke 6:46) In other words, listening is good but it's not enough. We have no right to call him 'Lord' if we never act on what he says. After the "coming in" there must always be a "going out." There's actually no such thing as passive faith.

Honestly, there are endless opportunities to absorb knowledge and information today. There are endless opportunities to be educated. We can attend infinite services and conferences. We can access literally millions of sermons over the internet or on satellite TV. We can access millions of books or articles in print or online. In this "Information Age" we are not starved of opportunities to hear teaching from the Bible. We are not starved of opportunities to be educated. But if all we do is absorb information, we're simply wasting our time and we're fooling ourselves. Even if we find really good teaching, it's useless unless there's a transition to action. We *must* apply what we're learning. This is the key difference between mere education and true discipleship.

In fact, true discipleship is closer to what we might call "mentoring" or "apprenticing" today. Jesus didn't establish a seminary, school or institution and then tell his disciples to come to lectures or classes three times a week. He didn't even establish a church building and tell them to come to services three times a week. It was much less formal than that. And it was much more proactive and practical than that. The disciples simply shadowed Jesus during every day life, going wherever he went, learning on the job. They learned by experience. They learned by doing. Jesus would give them an example to follow and then say, "now you try." He required them to get their hands dirty. He demanded that they act on what he was telling them. Jesus wasn't just giving them an education; he was giving them a whole new way to live. Indeed, before Christians were called Christians, they were simply called followers of *The Way*. It was a lifestyle. As Jesus imparted *The Way* to them He walked and talked with them daily. He hung out with them. He ate with them and cooked for them. He used the naturally occurring events of daily life as opportunities to teach important allegorical principles. He gave them goals to achieve. He also led by example. When he wanted to teach his disciples about humility he literally got down on his hands and knees and washed their feet. He didn't ask them to do anything he wasn't willing to do himself. In that way he proved his integrity to them. He prayed for them. They became close friends because of the time they spent together as a group. Jesus personally made sure that each of them were trained, equipped and empowered to become leaders themselves one day and when that day came he told them to go make disciples of their own, putting into practice everything they had learned from him. He did this so that their disciples could make disciples of their own, who could then make disciples of their own, who could make disciples of their own...and so on. It was a self-replicating system whereby each disciple would be proactively trained to go out, engage in Kingdom work and be able to lead others to Christ.

This self-replicating method of discipleship had two incredible benefits.

## BENEFIT 1 - EXPLOSIVE GROWTH

Let's say the original twelve disciples obeyed Jesus' command to make disciples of their own and each mentored a new group of twelve. Then imagine each of those new twelve were empowered to make twelve of their own, and so on. Within just four cycles of disciples making disciples, the original twelve would have multiplied into almost a quarter of a million disciples of Christ.

12 x 12 x 12 x 12 x 12 = 248,832

If each of those 248,832 went out to make twelve disciples of their own, there would then be 3 million disciples. If each of the 3 million made twelve disciples of their own, there would be 35 million disciples. If the 35 million did likewise, there would then be 420 million. Imagine 420 million disciples actively going out to impact their communities as Jesus and the first twelve had done. Disciples making disciples making disciples. You can see how Christianity spread like wildfire during the early years of the church. The growth was exponential. And since Jesus proved it only takes three years to turn a group of ordinary fishermen and tax collectors into fully-trained disciple-makers, each one could actually have had mentored many, many groups in their lifetime.

Remember how the writer to the Hebrews chastised them for keeping their teaching milky? At least part of the reason for his frustration was that they were slowing down this system of self-replicating discipleship. He says, *"You have been believers so long now **that you ought to be teaching others.**"* (Heb 5:12) It was expected that believers could eventually be teachers of others, who could be teachers of others, who could be teachers of others. By keeping the teaching milky, they were never maturing to that point.

Not only is this kind of growth staggering but it's persecution-proof. When Jesus left the earth, he left behind at least twelve disciples to carry on the work. It didn't matter that Jesus had gone in physical body because the twelve were more than ready to lead themselves. When each of those twelve disciples were dead, they would have left behind at least twelve of their own disciples to carry on the work too - which would be 144 disciples overall. It didn't matter that the twelve had gone because the 144 were more than ready to lead as well. Similarly, when any one of those 144 were martyred, they each left behind at least twelve of their own - 1,728 disciples overall. It didn't matter that the 144 weren't there in body anymore because the 1,728 they left behind were more than ready to lead themselves. In other words, every time the authorities came to jail or kill a Christian disciple-maker, the work would continue unabated through those he had trained. His disciples would just continue making disciples of their own. It's a bit like the Hydra myth where the beast couldn't be harmed by violence because every time a head was cut off, several more would appear in its place. Every time a Christian leader is cut off, there should be a legacy of at least 12 who will keep the work going and growing. The constant dissemination of responsibility to others makes the church impervious to violence. Take the buildings and the leaders away and it won't matter because there will always be others who know how to lead and disciple. This is why the New Testament church grew in spite of persecution in the first century and it's why the Chinese church has grown from 2 million to 80 million in the face of persecution today.

This is something we must remember then. The goal of a Christian leader is not to create dependent followers who will fall apart without him. The goal of a Christian leader is to do such a good job that he eventually renders himself obsolete. Think of it like parenting. The ultimate goal of a parent is not to create children who will be dependent on them for the rest of their lives. That's parental failure. The ultimate goal of a parent is to empower their child with such wisdom and maturity that they can be parents of their own kids one day. So that those kids can become parents of their own. So that their kids can become parents of their own etc. This is the system by which the general population grows and it should be the system by which the church grows. Don't create followers; create more leaders.

## Benefit 2 - Deep Growth

This system doesn't just produce unstoppable numbers; the small group discipleship format was, and remains, the most effective method by which to produce deep, strong, enduring and determined faith too. The Master knew what he was doing. These weren't passive pew warmers coming out the other side of this discipleship system. These were people who had been mentored daily, intimately, intensively and who, as part of their training, were expected to step out in obedience, putting their faith and reputations on the line for God's Kingdom. It was because they had learned by practical application that they quickly became empowered to teach the Gospel, defend the faith, make converts, feed the hungry, help the poor, heal the sick and cast out demons. Jesus' words were not just classroom theory to these disciples. They were experienced veterans who had seen action. In fact, for them, faith in those words had often been the difference between life and death.

Remember when Jesus sent out the 12 and then the 72, he told them, *"Take nothing for your journey...Don't take a walking stick, a traveller's bag, food, money, or even a change of clothes. Wherever you go, stay in the same house until you leave town."* (Luke 9:3-4) The disciples might well have thought, "Woah now, wait a minute! All these nice ideals you've been telling us about are all very well but you're now expecting us to put this into action? No money? No food? How are we going to eat? How are we going to survive? Where will we sleep?" The rubber was really hitting the road here. They were about to physically go out into hostile territory with nothing to live on but faith. You can imagine there was a certain amount of trepidation about this before they went.

Yet, go they did. And when the 72 returned to report back to Jesus you can hear the excitement in their voices: *"Lord, even the demons obey us when we use your name!"* (Luke 10:17) Of course, Jesus had been telling them this all along but the difference now was they'd put the theory into practice and experienced it for themselves. You can hear the increased faith in their words: "*Wow! This actually works! He wasn't just giving us nice sounding ideals. We did what Jesus told us to do...and it worked! Jesus really is who he says he is!"* Because they were seeing the reality of Jesus' words in action, their faith soared. And with that increased faith, they were ready to now attempt even greater things. They were slowly turning from lambs into lions. They collectively swept through Asia and Europe with all the power of a tornado. Nothing, but *nothing*, could turn these people back. Indeed, they were turning into the kind of men who would eventually give up their very lives for Jesus. All because they were obedient enough to "go".

Bored? Restless? Disengaged? These were words that just didn't apply to the early church. Scared? Yes. Persecuted? Yes. Excited? Yes. But life was never dull. They were on a white-knuckle ride which was simultaneously terrifying and thrilling. They were literally changing the world. Much of our restlessness exists simply because we have refused to get on that white-knuckle ride of active, practical faith and have instead chosen a safe life of passive inertia.

But get on it we must. We must get back to true discipleship.

The work of the church must no longer be in the hands of a few professionals at the top of a hierarchy but instead must be constantly disseminated to the hands and feet of the entire church who are empowered and sent out to act. Church must no longer solely be about formal ceremonies, classes, services and rituals. Perhaps it must no longer be about those things at all. I don't see many of those things in the New Testament. What I do see is a daily way of life where each member is empowered because they have learned not just by hearing the word, but by being compelled to be doers also.

This type of deep discipleship can only be done effectively in small groups. Just as one married couple can only parent a small number of children effectively before they are spread too thin, and just as one teacher can only teach a small class of children effectively before they are spread too thin, and just as one army commander can only lead a small platoon of soldiers before he is spread too thin, a Christian leader can only effectively train a small group of disciples before he is spread too thin. Jesus demonstrated that if you really want to disciple people, you have to get alongside them, get to know them, develop friendships with them, develop a bond of trust with them and develop accountability with them. It's impossible for one man to disciple hundreds because it's barely possible for one man to know that many names. So again, responsibility to lead needs to be disseminated and more leaders constantly raised up to mentor individual groups.

Remember, Peter called all believers a *"royal priesthood"* who are *all* equipped to show others the goodness of God (1 Peter 2:9). Under the Old Testament system in Israel there was a professional priestly class who were appointed to represent God to the people and everything was centred around them and the Temple, but under the New Covenant we *all* now have that responsibility to represent God to the world and we're to *go* out with it. There should not be this division between clergy and laity in the modern church. As someone once said, the relatively recent invention of "laymen" has only succeeded in producing "lame men." As a kingdom of priests we all have work to do. We all have ways to lead in accordance with our gifts. In the early history of the church there was never any suggestion that one could come to passively watch a show on Sunday every week and do nothing more. That was not church then and it still isn't church today.

# The Negative Impact Of Mere Education Over True Discipleship

As James told us, hearing without applying is a waste of time. But not only is it futile, it can actually lead to counter-productive results. Apart from the restlessness, boredom and lack of spiritual progress that we've already explored, there are a couple of other problems that I want to mention.

The first is pride.

Derek Prince writes, *"If we were to go to theological seminary or a Bible school and sit for three years in classes we would get a lot of head knowledge. What does that knowledge do? It puffs up. Jesus didn't do that. He made his disciples follow behind Him and serve Him. If we don't combine training with serving, we are going to produce the wrong results. The only safeguard against giving people knowledge is enabling them to serve."*

Knowledge by itself puffs up. It leads to pride. This is a dangerous thing. Paul writes to the Corinthians, *"we know that "all of us possess knowledge." This "knowledge" puffs up, but love builds up."* (1 Cor 8:1) Ironically, and tragically, some of the most knowledgeable people about the Bible are the most arrogant. You have probably seen them. They have turned their faith into nothing more than an intellectual pursuit. All they do is argue with one another about finer points of theological doctrine and their verbal duels quickly turn into ugly games of one-upmanship where both sides are unwilling to back down because their pride is on the line. They don't argue from love; they argue to win the argument. They have come to believe that the sole aim of Christian life is just to be...right. Sitting cloistered in their studies, surrounded by books and commentaries, they know where to find verses in a finger-click, but they've become self-righteous, condemnatory and cold. Matthew Thiessen succinctly put it, *"sometimes, as we grow smarter, our heart grows harder."*

Of course, this isn't to say you shouldn't read anymore. Quite the opposite. Acquire as much knowledge as you can. But as we learn we must also learn to *apply*. Paul wrote to Timothy saying, *"All Scripture is breathed out by God and profitable for teaching, for reproof, for correction, and for training in righteousness, that the man of God may be complete,* **equipped for every good work.***"* (2 Tim 3:16-17). We learn to be equipped for good *work*. Not for the sake of just knowing things. Jesus didn't appoint professors; he appointed followers.

It is only when one is forced out into the world to turn that theoretical head knowledge into practical acts of love and kindness; to make contact with real human beings; to serve them; to love them; to meet them face-to-face; share the Gospel with them; to get our hands dirty; share their sorrows and struggles; enduring the scorn and persecution along the way; that we firstly actually do any good in the world, but secondly, that we learn compassion and humility to counter-act the real risk of pride in our own lives. In other words, our own sanctification happens as we minister to others. You're helping them but you're also helping yourself at the same time. Melody Green said, *"The question is this - once you are right...then what? Do you just sit around in your "rightness", or do you seek God's direction to see how and where you can be used most effectively for the Kingdom of God? What the world is dying for is hundreds and thousands of believers who are determined to see the lost find out who their Creator is before they stand before Him on that great and awesome day."*

It's been said that people don't care how much you know until they know how much you care. Practical acts of love and kindness break down barriers in our attempts to reach the world while simultaneously keeping us humble. It's a win-win combination.

A second negative consequence of failing to apply the Word of God is that we tend to forget what we've learned if we don't. James writes, *"For if you listen to the word and don't obey, it is like glancing at your face in a mirror. You see yourself, walk away, and forget what you look like."* (James 1:23-24) This verse reminds me of a saying that all trainee teachers in the UK are told at University: *"I hear and I forget. I see and I remember. I do and I understand."* If we only hear something but never do anything with it, we tend to walk away and forget it rather quickly. To prove this point, think back over the past year and count how many sermons you still vividly remember. Sometimes I've honestly forgotten what a Sunday sermon was by lunch time! And that's nothing to do with the quality of the sermon; it's just the way we're wired.

If we see something with our own eyes, it tends to stick longer in the memory. For better or worse, images stay with us. And so visualisation really helps. This is perhaps why Jesus taught so often with parables - stories conjure mental images in our mind that we don't easily forget. If I were to say the words, "Hansel and Gretel", "Snow White and the Seven Dwarves" or "Goldilocks and the Three Bears", I can guarantee that mental images just flashed through your mind that help you remember those stories. Some of those mental images may even be rooted as far back as your early childhood. Bible stories stand out in the memory for the same reason. Indeed, if I try to remember the most memorable teaching from my church over the past few years I don't think of sermons as much as I think of a couple of powerful drama sketches.

But as the saying suggests, if we really want deep *understanding* of a thing, we have to go beyond both hearing and seeing and actively get involved with it. We have to apply ourselves to it directly. At that point we begin to move beyond mere knowledge and into wisdom.

Hopefully we're beginning to realise all the advantages of small-group, practical discipleship. Hopefully we're beginning to understand that church is as much about "going out" as it is "coming in."

> *"Jesus Christ lived in the midst of his enemies. At the end all his disciples deserted him. On the Cross he was utterly alone, surrounded by evildoers and mockers. For this cause he had come, to bring peace to the enemies of God. So the Christian, too, belongs not in the seclusion of a cloistered life but in the thick of foes. There is his commission, his work.* <u>*'The kingdom is to be in the midst of your enemies.*</u> *And he who will not suffer this does not want to be of the Kingdom of Christ; he wants to be among friends, to sit among roses and lilies, not with the bad people but the devout people. O you blasphemers and betrayers of Christ! If Christ had done what you are doing who would ever have been spared' (Luther)."* - Dietrich Bonhoeffer

# Chapter 4
# We Have Become Too Comfortable

*"The church is not a dormitory for sleepers, it is an institution for workers; it is not a rest camp, it is a front line trench." - Billy Sunday*

---

Why did we lose the "going out" aspect of Christianity? Because we decided that we loved our comfort more. As Western society grew in wealth it became able to supply its own material needs and comfort and easy-living became its ultimate goal. We started dreaming of a future where a better life meant an easier life. A life where our domestic chores and personal grooming would be carried out by robots, where technology would make work unnecessary and where travel would be possible with zero effort.

This cultural striving for the easy life spread into the church and instead of preaching about the need to pick up your cross, walk the difficult narrow path, evangelise, confront evil, deal with persecution and scorn in the public arena etc., pastors started preaching about a God who was simply there to help people towards the fulfilment of the cultural dream. A God who existed to make us healthier, wealthier, happier and who would fast-track us to the life of ease we craved. Because these pastors told us what we wanted to hear, we gave them our support and made megastars out of them.

The more we achieved the comfort, the less we thought we needed that genie style God. If God existed only to provide us with luxury, once we had those things, what else did we need him for? He could go back in his bottle. We became complacent and spiritually apathetic. Comfort always breeds apathy. That apathy led to passive inertia and inertia led to lukewarm faith, weakness, timidity and in the end, boredom and restlessness. We lost true discipleship because true discipleship, with all its nerve-jangling practical application, necessarily involves risk, danger and costly self-sacrifice. Things we decided we could do without.

Most modern churches have been affected by this mindset and therefore, they will provide very little impetus towards "going out." You'll be given plenty of opportunities to attend classes, Bible studies, services, conferences, sermons...in fact, anything insular. Anything that lends itself to comfortable, passive attendance. But you will rarely, if ever, be driven out of your comfort-zone. You will rarely, if ever, be personally apprenticed in those things. It's very easy for a modern Christian to come and watch a show on Sunday, stay anonymous in the crowd for the duration, and then disappear for the rest of the week without putting into practice anything that they've learned. I know because I've done it. Christian leaders no longer send out or demand anything from you because if there's one thing that the modern leader hates to make anyone feel, it's uncomfortable.

Indeed, most of what you see in church today is designed for comfort. Comfortable chairs. Comfortable sanctuary. Comfortable air temperature. Often a comfortable message too. When churches no longer try to grow by venturing out into a dangerous and hostile world with an uncompromising message, the only alternative is to grow by putting on the most entertaining show to draw a crowd and then making the surroundings as comfortable as possible so the crowd will have no reason to leave. A comfort trap is the aim. It's an appeal to our ultimate desire. The success of the comfort trap is then defined by how many bottoms there are on seats on a Sunday morning. In order to make the experience as "sticky" as possible, money is poured into increasing the entertainment values. New plush sanctuaries, jumbotron screens, multimedia packages, lighting rigs, sound systems, soft furnishings, cafes with vanilla-mocha-frappa-latte-cappuccinos... and anything else that will enhance the show. In a "go" culture, this is money that would save lives, feed hungry mouths, clothe naked backs and provide warm shelters for the homeless. But because we don't want to go to them and are stuck in our inward facing culture, we would rather create ostentatious palaces full of creature comforts than directly help the lost and most broken in society wherever they are. And again, from a pastor's perspective, keeping people comfortable so that they'll never want to leave often means compromised, ear-tickling sermons, prosperity doctrine and the avoidance of controversial issues. Exhortations that thundered from the lips of godly men in history now come delivered as watered-down pandering suggestions from the pulpit today, if at all. Indeed, you'll often hear this made clear from the platform: *"We don't want to make anyone feel uncomfortable here today..."*

Why not? The Christian message isn't comfortable. It never has been.

We get this wrong from the start. Have you ever been to an evangelistic service where the pastor preaches milk and then closes by asking everyone to bow their heads and close their eyes? Then he says, *"while every head is bowed and every eye is closed, if you want to give your life to the Lord just raise your hand where you are. We don't want to make you feel uncomfortable. No one is going to see you."* As people slip up their hands, teams of ushers sneak silently about the sanctuary like ninjas to put a welcome pack into their hands. What kind of message does that send? It tells them that faith can be personal, insular, hidden, private and comfortable...when it cannot. Jesus has a much more uncomfortable message for anyone who wants to enter his kingdom. He says, *"Everyone who acknowledges me publicly here on earth, I will also acknowledge before my Father in heaven. But everyone who denies me here on earth, I will also deny before my Father in heaven." (Matt 10:32-33)* In other words, if someone isn't ready to stand up and acknowledge Christ when people are looking, then they're not ready to be a Christian at all. And if we can't stand up and be counted even amongst the converted, what chance do we have of doing it amongst the unconverted when it really matters?

Jesus was, in general, far less interested in making people feel comfortable than the average modern pastor. When he sent out his twelve disciples he told them, *"If you refuse to pick up your cross and follow me, you are not worthy of being mine"*. He continued, *"If you cling to your life, you will lose it; but if you give up your life for me, you will find it." (Matt 10:38-39)* Jesus was sending them out and telling them, *"following my commands isn't optional. If you aren't willing to pick up your cross and go, you're not worthy of me. And if you're not obedient, you have no right to call me 'Lord'."* At no point does Jesus pretend that a true walk of faith is comfortable. In fact, he's quite explicit about it being very *uncomfortable*. He goes so far as to say, *"look, you might actually be required to die for me. People are going to hate you that much. It isn't going to be easy. But that's the narrow road you must walk."* This is Jesus' message throughout the Gospels and we see the reality of it throughout the entire New Testament. Christians being mocked, hated, persecuted, beaten and even stoned and put to death. Yet this is what true discipleship looks like. It's walking that narrow road. It's learning to apply what you've heard in spite of the opposition from a hostile world.

We must get back to that, and in doing so, renounce comfort as our ultimate goal. Instead, we must once again learn to embrace risk as the theme of our lives. We must once again be willing to go out to a hostile world proclaiming an uncompromising message. We must once again regard our reputations and even our lives as naught compared to the mission which Jesus has set before us. As we bring light into dark places we must embrace the demands, the danger, the confrontation and the risks that it necessarily entails. Yes, it will be scary, yes there will be persecution, yes it will be exciting and yes it will be life-changing....yes, it will even be *world*-changing. This is what New Testament Christianity looks like. There's simply no other way.

Former megachurch pastor, Francis Chan, admitted that all you really need to draw a crowd is a charismatic speaker, an attractive building, a decent sound system, some good marketing, child care facilities and a cosy environment. If you put on the best show in town you'll get the numbers. But that isn't church. It's nothing like what we read about in the New Testament. And it doesn't produce real disciples. It produces sanctuaries full of false converts who are there for an entertaining show but who balk at the idea of risk, danger, obedience and persecution for Christ because that's not what they signed up for. They signed up for a cosy Christian country club; they didn't sign up for embarrassment and scorn. The "come" culture produces weak, passive attendees rather than active, highly trained disciples.

Sure, many of these churches look successful on the surface because they have that big crowd and they make a lot of money, but often they're spiritually hollow shells. They're like the churches of Sardis and Laodicea in Revelation. When Jesus writes to the church in Sardis he says that they have a reputation amongst men for being alive but they are in fact, dead. To the church in Laodicea he writes that they have a lot of wealth and comfort but it's made them apathetic, lukewarm and worthy to be spat out of his mouth. Both of these churches are successful to human eyes but Jesus' opinion is very different. In other words, full sanctuaries, full collection plates and full programs are not necessarily the signs of spiritual health. For proof of that fact you only have to consider that the largest church in America is Joel Osteen's Lakewood Church in Houston, Texas.

I've often fantasised about a congregation arriving at church one Sunday morning, expecting the usual service routine, only to be told that this week the doors would be closed and they would be sent out in teams to evangelise and work in the local community instead. Wouldn't that be exciting? I've often wondered though, how many people would stick around in such an event. And how many would silently sneak away to an early lunch. And how many would never return at all to a church that actually expects them to move out of their comfort zones. It remains just a fantasy for me because I've never actually witnessed it. I honestly don't know if many pastors would be willing to make such demands of their congregation. Perhaps from fear of losing members. Perhaps even from fear of losing the income those members provide. Such is the professional nature of the church today with its salaries and building maintenance costs. But in the meantime, it's just too easy for us to remain insular, hidden behind four walls, going through the motions, acquiring head knowledge, bickering about the minutiae of it, but never *doing* anything with it. It might be easy, but it's not true faith. It's not true discipleship. It isn't what Jesus requires of us. We must apply.

## We Have Become Fearful

The lust for comfort has not only bred apathy; it's bred fear too.

As we look out from behind our four walls, we can't help but notice that Satan is laying waste to the world. Secularism is stomping on everything we believe; we see evolutionists disparaging the Biblical account of creation; we see pop culture filling up with Satanic influences; we see laws being perverted to permit immorality; we see comedians casually mocking our Saviour on television; we see anti-Christian worldviews brainwashing the minds of our friends and neighbours through the media; we see the world heading for moral decay and ultimately ruin, and because we've never gone out to confront it, we have started to believe that Satan and his minions are an irresistible force. The enemy bombards us daily with propaganda to that effect and we have started to internalise the lie that his advance is too strong and that we could not defeat him, even if we tried. A feeling of hopelessness has begun to set in and we have become timid.

It will only be when we leave the comfort of the four walls, go to battle, fight the good fight, put our faith to the test, in the middle of the culture, influencing it, confronting it, changing it, that we will discover, like the 72 did, that even demons would obey us when we use Jesus' name. It will only be when we go to battle that we will realise just how much power we have available to us through the power of the Holy Spirit. Indeed, the Bible tells us that the same power that raised Jesus from the dead lives in us (Rom 8:11). Somehow that's still just words to us. We've never experienced the reality of it and so we're not sure we can really stake our lives on it. Yet Jesus insists that we take him at his word and the entire New Testament confirms that through us, this same power would change the world. If we would *just try*. Our transition from lambs to lions would come in the same way that it came for the first disciples - through going out and putting Jesus' words into practice in the middle of a fallen culture.

I must be very clear that when I use the Biblical terms, "go to battle" and "fight the good fight", in no way do I mean, or does the Bible mean, literal violence. I mean in the way demonstrated by the early church. I mean we must preach the gospel in public, be visible with our good deeds, when someone is mocking Jesus, to speak up in defence. When abortion or infanticide is being promoted, that we be the voice to the voiceless and defend their right to life. When our governments try to strip freedoms away, that we protest and petition for all that is good and just. That when we see children or animals being mistreated, we intervene. That when we see someone hurting, we give them comfort. That when we see someone without money, we give them some of ours. That when our friends or family are intent on some form of immoral behaviour, we guide them away from it. That when people mock and hate us, we bless them and pray for them and give them nothing but love in return. I mean that the church must mobilise itself, stand up and speak up, and make sure that truth, hope, love and justice is given a voice in society.

Satan knows that we would defeat him if we got our act together and so he relies on stoking our apathy and fear to keep us inactive, insular, passive, weak and timid. Pastors actually aid Satan's cause when they refuse to mobilise the church and send them out like Jesus did. Pastors aid Satan's cause when they say, *"I don't want you to feel uncomfortable. You just sit and listen to me talk for a few hours and get excited about it. That's doing your bit. That's what Christianity is all about."* #

Look at the world. Social decay is increasing noticeably. Humanistic agendas are being pushed in moral, political and social levels in schools. Homosexuality, relativism, false religion and cults, corruption, greed, occultism and inhumanity is thriving and going largely unopposed. While the church should be riding out to stand in bold opposition, defending the truth and exposing the corruption and lies - knowing that the gates of hell cannot prevail against us - we are instead sitting comfortably secluded in our sanctuaries, encouraged to do so by many pastors, spending all our time splitting doctrinal hairs, getting puffed up about it, playing a religion game, drinking tea and coffee and talking about the colour of the new carpet.

Society's conscience cannot be pricked by the Gospel because it's simply not hearing it. We should be shouting it from the rooftops. It should be sweeping the world like a tornado in the same way it did in New Testament times. But there is very little threat to evil coming from the church today. The secular world doesn't need to be wary of a church that sits idly by, pampering itself with creature comforts and which doesn't force itself to take daring risks for the Gospel. The secular world is free to pursue its agenda, mock the truth, chip away at freedoms, and claim more converts for itself. It is safe from a cowering and complacent Christianity. And so the world deteriorates.

# Chapter 5
## We're Active But Not Productive

*"An inwardly focused church is an unhealthy church. It is a dying church. Biblically, a church that fails to look at the world around it is no church at all."* - Francis Chan

*"You shall not find any Christian community that has flourished after it has become negligent of the outside world."* - Charles Spurgeon

---

Our unwillingness to leave the comfort of our sanctuary can mean that even our activity becomes inwardly focused and therefore lacks real productivity. John Wimber rightly said, *"Many times people who attend Church can become more focused on what's happening in Church than the reason behind why the Church exists. The Church is not the building, its the people; its not just the gathering, its also the scattering."*

We can become consumed with activities that perpetuate the church machinery but don't ever get around to the reason for the church's existence. It's like a farmer who is constantly fixing and polishing his tractor in the barn but who never actually gets round to ploughing a field with it. He's busy alright but he's lost sight of what the tractor is for and there are no crops to show for all the effort. An inwardly focused church is actually rarely short of things to do, should you wish to "get involved."

Our insular services, events and conferences, after all, need band rehearsals and meetings. We need car park attendants.

And a welcoming team. And stewards. And sound engineers. And we need to print t-shirts and order name tags and lanyards for the ushers. There's a crèche rota and Sunday School rota. A rota for floral displays. We organise lunches, coffee mornings, arts and crafts fairs, bake sales and fellowship weekends away. There are building fund-raisers, church picnics and barbecues. And there's no shortage of administration for all this and no lack of emails to write or people to call. All these things and more create a great feeling of busyness, bustle and activity but in the end analysis all we're really doing is perpetuating the church machinery so that the church machinery can be perpetuated. We're still not actually ploughing or planting or harvesting and there are few crops to show for all the effort. We're still behind the four walls of the barn. We're still not fulfilling the Great Commission. Oswald J Smith said, *"Oh my friends, we are loaded with countless church activities, while the real work of the church, that of evangelising and winning the lost is almost entirely neglected."*

I have talked to many people who have delved into this kind of church involvement, joining rotas and loading themselves with the numerous church programs that are available. Often they report that they dread Sundays because it is one of the most stressful and busy days of the week! No longer is it a time for refreshment and encouragement with other believers as it was in the early church. They reach Sunday evenings exhausted and longing for another day to recover before starting work the next morning! A lot of this stress has come about because the church has moved from an *organic* to *organisational* form. The early church was marked by simplicity, informality, being Holy Spirit led, spontaneity, authenticity, honesty; today it's marked by formality, programs, rotas, staged events and shows. In economic terms, this turning of church into an organisation or institution has made it a 'high input, low output' system. In other words, our events, programs and buildings are very resource hungry and require a lot of time, organisational talent, administrative bureaucracy and money which can be quite exhausting, but there's very little discernible benefit from all the activity coming out the other side in the way of discipleship. i.e. changed lives.

This is a parable that may well describe our church experience:

*"They were surrounded by streams and lakes full of hungry fish. They met regularly to discuss the call to fish, the abundance of fish, and the thrill of catching fish. They got excited about fishing!*

*Someone suggested that they needed a philosophy of fishing, so they carefully defined and redefined fishing, and the purpose of fishing. They developed fishing strategies and tactics. Then they realised that they had been going at it backwards. They had approached fishing from the point of view of the fisherman, and not from the point of view of the fish. How do fish view the world? How does the fisherman appear to the fish? What do fish eat, and when? These are all good things to know. So they began research studies, and attended conferences on fishing. Some travelled to faraway places to study different kinds of fish with different habits. Some got doctorates in fishology. But no one had yet gone fishing.*

*So a committee was formed to send out fishermen. As prospective fishing places outnumbered fishermen, the committee needed to determine priorities. A priority list of fishing places was posted on bulletin boards in all of the fellowship halls. But still, no one was fishing. A survey was launched to find out why. Most did not answer the survey, but from those who did, it was discovered that some felt called to study fish, a few to furnish fishing equipment, and several to go around encouraging the fishermen. What with meetings, conferences, and seminars, they just simply didn't have time to fish.*

*Now, Jake was a newcomer to the Fisherman's Fellowship. After one stirring meeting of the Fellowship, he went fishing and caught a large fish. At the next meeting, he told his story and was honoured for his catch. He was told that he had a special "gift of fishing." He was then scheduled to speak at all the Fellowship chapters and tell how he did it.*

*With all the speaking invitations and his election to the board of directors of the Fisherman's Fellowship, Jake no longer had time to go fishing. But soon he began to feel restless and empty. He longed to feel the tug on the line once again. So he cut the speaking, he resigned from the board, and he said to a friend, "Let's go fishing." They did, just the two of them, and they caught fish. The members of the Fisherman's Fellowship were many, the fish were plentiful, but the fishers were few!"* (Anonymous)

This parable highlights the fact that we are often full of activity but very little *productivity*. We're fishers who don't fish. In fact, quite often all these activities and programs that we initiate are just avoidance tactics. We don't want to do the simple but scary thing that really needs to be done so instead we talk about it, have meetings about it, plan conferences and seminars about it, sing songs about it, memorise verses about it, devise philosophies about it, create time-consuming organisational structures around it, do doctorate studies about it, develop strategies and tactics about it...so that we don't have to get out there and actually do it! In this way we stay busy but we retain our valued comfort. Comfortable Busyness: We feel this is the perfect combination.

## COMFORTABLE BUSYNESS

One of the outworkings of *comfortable busyness* is the way the church has become accustomed to tackling every issue, not by actually tackling the issue, but by holding an event *about* tackling the issue...so that we don't actually have to physically go and tackle the issue. We give these events cool titles like "Impact", "Imagine", "Breathe", "Glow", "Velocity" or "Unite". There we'll be told we're going to "lift his name high", "declare his name over the city", "sing for his glory" and other such things. We get a venue, a band, a sound system, a lighting rig, a "gifted communicator" and we put on a show. We'll put a whole lot of time and effort into making this thing happen and we'll whip up a great stir over it. "Something epic is going to happen! You don't want to miss this! God is going to show up!" On the night the crowd will hear a lot about "turning our city upside down", "seeing lives transformed" and "impacting our community." Everyone will get pumped up by the hyperbolic proclamations rolling down off the stage. There will be whoops, whistles and loud "Amens" as the crowd are told how big and great and able God is. Many will studiously scribble away on notepads as the key points come up on the big screen. Because we've made a worshipful noise "in this place tonight" we feel like we've really achieved something here. We feel like our passionate cries and air punches and songs of ecstasy must have really terrorised Satan. We even talk about having pulled down strongholds and having shaken the heavenlies with our praise. We think the thousands of dollars/euros/pounds that it cost to hire the venue, equipment and staff is money well spent because Satan is now surely scampering off in fear. And then everyone leaves the building telling one another about how "challenged" or "inspired" they felt.

And *nothing* is different. Nothing.

We go back to our normal lives. We more than likely won't look at those sermon notes again, let alone work out how to apply them to ourselves or our communities. The city wasn't turned upside down. And few lives, if any, were transformed. In time we'll forget the event even happened.

You see, all our words were just empty rhetoric. We had no intention of actually doing something to back it up. We're all bark and no bite. And Satan knows it. We really do believe God is great and able to do anything...but don't expect us to actually act in faith on that. We really do believe that God could transform lives...but don't expect us to actually talk to broken people about Jesus. We really do leave the event feeling challenged...but don't expect us to actually rise to that challenge.

Our Christian lives then can become characterised merely by a series of events, Sunday services, meetings, gatherings and conferences where we go in and talk a good game but where there's little practical application in between. The events are fun. They're cosy. We see our friends there. They're entertaining and often spectacular. They feel good. But I must keep referring to James - when there's no transition to action, they're ultimately a waste of time. We're deceiving ourselves if we go through these motions but never actually apply what we're learning or singing about.

Deep down we know this. Deep down we start to feel the futility of these events when there is no follow-through. Because almost always, you'll notice these events and conferences tend to have short life-spans. Once the initial novelty wears off and people start to realise nothing truly productive is coming from them, and that they're basically just grander, more expensive versions of what goes on in church every week, interest tends to diminish and attendance figures wane. Most annual Christian conferences and festivals won't last beyond their tenth birthday.

## Worship

Now one might say, "to have thousands of people united in worship of God is worth any amount of administration, time and money!" But this is to misunderstand what worship actually is. Worship is not, as it is characterised today, people coming to a holy place on a holy day at a holy hour to participate in a holy ritual led by a holy man dressed in holy clothes. It's not a performance-oriented enterprise at all. God says in Isaiah 1:

*"When you come to worship me, who asked you to parade through my courts with all your ceremony? Stop bringing me your meaningless gifts; the incense of your offerings disgusts me! As for your celebrations of the new moon and the Sabbath and your special days for fasting— they are all sinful and false. I want no more of your pious meetings. I hate your new moon celebrations and your annual festivals. They are a burden to me. I cannot stand them! When you lift up your hands in prayer, I will not look. Though you offer many prayers, I will not listen, for*

*your hands are covered with the blood of innocent victims. Wash yourselves and be clean! Get your sins out of my sight. Give up your evil ways. Learn to do good. Seek justice. Help the oppressed. Defend the cause of orphans. Fight for the rights of widows. "Come now, let's settle this," says the LORD. "Though your sins are like scarlet, I will make them as white as snow. Though they are red like crimson, I will make them as white as wool. If you will only obey me...."* Isaiah 1

God here is addressing a nation who were coming to the Temple in the time-honoured tradition, going through the time-honoured motions of worship, putting on a show of religion, making a great noise, saying all the right words and singing all the right songs, making a show of their piety and making bold claims about their devotion and love of God, but who were then living their daily lives in a way that didn't honour Him. Their actions weren't matching up. They weren't applying. They thought that if they said the right words at Temple their job was done. But this is the very definition of hypocrisy - *"the practice of verbally claiming to have moral standards or beliefs to which one's own behaviour does not conform."* It's mere pretence. A hollow facade. The people of Israel had this appearance of spirituality but their ceremonies had become hypocritical, false and even sinful in God's eyes because they weren't following through with their actions.

And in this passage in Isaiah God is saying, "*Enough with the pretence. Enough with noisy songs and promises of devotion. Enough with the pious meetings. Let me see some action. Let me see the reality of all these things you're telling me. Your worship to me is not the songs that you sing; it's in the way you live your lives. Learn to do good. Seek justice. Help the oppressed.* **Do** *something."* Worship isn't an event for an hour in a church or conference hall; it's a lifestyle. It's is in our every-day obedience to him. It's to be a daily follower of *The Way*. God absolutely despises our pious meetings, Sunday services and ceremonial worship if the words we say and the promises we make are not backed up by what we do. He considers it sinful and false and disgusting!

Dietrich Bonhoeffer wrote, *"Sometimes we don't need another chance to express how we feel or to ask someone to understand our situation. Sometimes we just need a firm kick in the pants. An unsmiling expectation that if we mean all these wonderful things we talk about and sing about, then lets see something to prove it."*

That could very well be God's message to the church in the West. He could very well say to us too, *"I'm sick of all your endless meetings and conferences, your noisy worship, the extravagant promises in the lyrics of your songs, your shows of piety...let me see something to prove it. No more conferences, events and seminars. No more avoidance tactics. At least not until you're ready to back up what you're saying with action. Go outside of the four walls and actually spread the Gospel, help the oppressed, defend orphans, fight for the cause of widows. **Do** something."*

## THE SONGS WE SING

Listen to the extravagant hyperbole in the lyrics of our worship songs. *"Lord I give you my heart, I give you my soul, I live for you alone." "I lay down my life and pick up my cross" "Lord, you are everything to me." "Jesus, we're living for your name, take it all." "Jesus, you're all I need." "I surrender all" "Refiner's fire, my heart's one desire is to be holy, set apart for you my Master, ready to do your will."* Worship songs are full of this hyperbole where we promise to give up everything for Christ and hand our entire lives over to him because he is our only and all-consuming passion. Then we walk out the door and get on with our lives like nothing has happened.

As we sing these songs with gusto and make these bold promises of devotion to God, how often do we take a moment to concentrate on what we're actually saying? Do we realise what we're promising to do? Do we realise Who we're making these promises to? Do we realise that God actually expects us to follow through on what we're saying? Do we realise what that would actually look like? We must be careful not to say things to God so flippantly if we do not mean them.

Solomon wrote, *"As you enter the house of God, keep your ears open and your mouth shut! Don't be a fool who doesn't realise that mindless offerings to God are evil. And don't make rash promises to God, for he is in heaven, and you are only here on earth. So let your words be few...when you make a promise to God, don't delay in following through, for God takes no pleasure in fools. Keep all the promises you make to him. It is better to say nothing than to promise something that you don't follow through on. In such cases, your mouth is making you sin...Dreaming all the time instead of working is foolishness. And there is ruin in a flood of empty words. Fear God instead."* (Ecclesiastes 5:1-2, 4-6 & 7)

AW Tozer said, *"Today we sing songs that are so dishonest that I sometimes hesitate to sing them. Yet when we sing the average hymn, if God Almighty compelled us to be entirely 100 percent honest, we simply could not sing them because their words would not be true of us…It is only by a charitable adaptation of the truth that we are able to sing most of the hymns we sing."*

The next time we leave a church event thinking, "wow, I felt really challenged by that message tonight" let us always ask the next question, "how do I intend to meet that challenge? How will I change henceforth? What will I **do**?" And then most of all, let us actually go out and do it. Otherwise the event will have just been an exercise in hypocrisy.

If we're not ready to follow through on the words of the songs, then let's not sing them. As Solomon wrote, *"It is better to say nothing than to promise something that you don't follow through on."* We get no brownie points for lying to God. Instead let's start talking honestly about *why* we're not ready to follow through on them and start working towards a place where we can. Let's start being authentic with God and with each other.

# Chapter 6
## We Have Lost Perspective

*"Preach abroad. It is the cooping yourselves up in rooms that has dampened the work of God, which never was and never will be carried out to any purpose without going into the highways and hedges and compelling men and women to come in."* - Jonathan Edwards

---

You may remember a TV show from a few years ago called "Big Brother" where people were locked away inside a house over a few months in summer. Every single area of the house was covered by cameras and microphones so that each housemate was monitored at all times. It was billed as a social experiment to see how people reacted when they were confined to a small space with absolutely no access to the outside world.

One of the most noticeable effects of being cooped up in this small compound, something which repeated itself in every season of the show, was that the housemates very quickly lost their sense of perspective on life. When the total extent of their world was reduced to four walls, the small things within those walls suddenly seemed like big issues.

They began getting into furious fights over a missing piece of fruit from the fruit bowl. Or a lost sock. Little gestures and stray words became magnified and blown out of all proportion. The boredom of an unoccupied mind meant they had nothing to do but gossip about other housemates and stew on conversations and arguments. Resentments simmered and often overflowed.

They created drama and tensions where there naturally should be none. And of course this is what the producers of the show wanted because it made for explosive television.

Every Friday night one of the housemates would be voted out and immediately after coming back into the outside world, they would sit down for an interview with the host and be shown footage from their time in the house. As they watched themselves back on screen they would shake their heads sheepishly and cringe at their behaviour, embarrassed that they had ever got so worked up about minute and insignificant things. They would protest that they didn't recognise the person on screen. It was as though they had been woken from a dream or snapped out of some state of hypnosis and could suddenly see how bizarrely petty and silly their disputes had been. Being back in the real world, even just for a few minutes, had suddenly put all those tiny issues back into perspective.

The minute they stepped outside of their compound, the screaming crowds reminded them that other people existed outwith those in their little group. They were suddenly made aware of a great big wide world again. A world in which grand themes had been taking place while they had been locked away. A world where wars had begun. Where people had died. Where new lives had begun. Where terrorists had struck. Where tsunamis and earthquakes had ravaged nations. Where economic crises had robbed people of their livelihoods and homes. Events of huge national and international significance had taken place. Things they hadn't heard about because all the while they had been shut up in a compound bickering about a missing banana or a pair of socks. How insignificant in the larger scheme of things that now seemed. How trivial. No wonder they felt so sheepish when they watched their behaviour back in that context.

A similar thing can happen in church.

When we lock ourselves away inside four walls and make church insular and small, we can lose perspective and that leads to arguments over things that are actually pretty trivial. I talked a little about this in *Stay Free*. We get into arguments about flower arrangements or bicker about how loud the drums were. Or whether it was right that one of the elders wasn't wearing a tie on Sunday. We argue endlessly about minor theological doctrines to no use or advantage other than to be proved right. We gossip about a guy because he raised his hands when he was singing or whisper about that lady in the fourth row that wore an unusual hat. We can often become self-righteous prigs, overly fussy and totally preoccupied with trivialities that really don't matter in the grand scheme of things. This kind of behaviour is repellent. And like the Big Brother contestants, I wonder what we'll do if we reach heaven and God shows us back a video of our lives. If we will suddenly come to our senses and feel embarrassed about these petty squabbles. If we will shake our heads and cringe at our behaviour because in making our world small, we lost perspective and spent our lives making mountains out of molehills.

It's not as though we don't have grand themes to be getting on with. It's not as though there isn't a great wide world out there to engage with.

It is estimated that 150,000 people die each day in the world and most of them don't know Jesus. That's perhaps one person, every second, of every day, being lost for all eternity. Jesus gave us the Great Commission to rescue them with the Gospel. Us. You. Me. There is no bigger theme than this. There is no bigger mission than this. It encompasses the entire planet. All peoples. In all the towns and cities and villages of the world. And all the jungles and desert places of the world. In all nations. On every continent. Go. Tell. Proclaim. Heal. Cast out demons. Confront evil. Oppose tyranny. Seek justice. Help the oppressed. Free captives. Change the face of the world. Alter eternities. Wow. We have no excuses for making our world small. We have so much work to do.

If we accept this massive challenge that Jesus has given us, broaden our horizons and work together in the world for the sake of God's kingdom, we will soon find the idle gossiping and ugly petty bickering that may characterise church life today coming to an end. We may discover that all the little, divisive things that may seem so important right now are put into proper perspective. Instead, as we tackle the big issues of life I believe we will develop an astonishing strength of unity.

Look at soldiers.

## BAND OF BROTHERS

Outside of the family unit, there is perhaps no company of people amongst whom you will find a greater sense of brotherhood, unity and belonging than soldiers. This develops because, as they go out from the relative safety of their base camp into the war zone, they know they are surrounded by hostile enemies and the only people they can really trust are the other members of their squad. More than that, they absolutely *must* trust the other members of their squad. They have a mission to complete and it is only achievable if they work together and stick together. They cannot do it alone. Their very lives are on the line every second of every minute of every hour of every day and they simply need one another just to stay alive.

The guy at the front of the platoon can only keep his eyes on what's ahead and he needs to trust that his team-mate on rear guard is alert to any danger from behind. If he's not switched on, there's a good chance he won't be going home alive. Likewise, the guy driving the tank has to hope that the gunners can shoot properly and the gunners have to trust the driver won't steer them off a cliff or into an ambush. Each of their lives are in the other's hands. They are each other's eyes and ears. They almost operate as a single organism composed of many interdependent parts, and they are all of one mind and focused on one mission. This interdependence on one another as they face down the enemy and overcome perilous situations creates an unparalleled sense of togetherness. They are a band of brothers.

We should find that same sense of unity in the church and for much the same reasons.

If the church left its base camp and went out into a hostile world, focused on its Great Commission, attacking the pagan godlessness and sinfulness, the greed, the materialism, occultism, demonic powers and faced the persecution, scorn, hatred and retaliation that would inevitably come their way, they would find they need to rely on one another to complete their mission and perhaps just to survive. They would need to operate as one unit, one mind and one heart in order to meet their objectives. Paul wrote to the Philippians saying, *"whether I come and see you again or only hear about you, I will know that you are standing together with one spirit and one purpose, fighting together for the faith, which is the Good News."* (Philippians 1:27) That should be a picture of the church today. Standing together, working together, fighting together, in aid of a common cause. So united should the church be that Paul even described the church as a single body made up of many parts saying each part of the body needs to work with the other parts to get the job done. We should really be like one organism. We must be each other's eyes and ears and hands and feet. And just as a human body develops muscles by work and resistance, so will the body of Christ. If you sit on the sofa and give your body no work it becomes flabby and weak. If you get to the gym and give it some resistance, it develops muscles. The body of Christ is the same. This is why the church historically thrives in the face of persecution. It gets stronger as it faces challenges.

Therefore the church needs to set achievable objectives - real objectives in the real world - it needs to be trained and equipped by discipleship to meet those objectives, and it needs to work together in unity towards those objectives. What are the problems and opportunities that exist in your local community? Identify them. Then train and send out groups to tackle them. Not only will the church then become more productive, but it will become stronger, more winsome and more unified. Our individual and collective sanctification will increase rapidly as we leave comfort zones to disciple and minister to others.

## SANCTIFICATION THROUGH MINISTRY

Here are a few examples of the ways we are made stronger through active ministry:

One way is that you will be driven into the Bible for answers and your knowledge of the Word will increase rapidly. Since starting the Fuel Project there have been many challenges from Atheists, Adventists, Mormons, Jehovah's Witnesses, Catholics, Muslims, Anti-Semites, Hebrew Roots Movement proponents and Satanists to name just a few groups. Every one of these people has had their own agenda, questions and problems and sometimes they have been completely unanticipated. Therefore, I've often found myself being driven to pore over the Scriptures for answers in previously unseen ways so that I can give a robust defence of the truth. The resistance they have provided has accelerated my sanctification through the Word and I've come to deeper understanding of various things.

Similarly, I've also had the privilege of being part of an introduction to Christianity course for international students over the past few years. These students, mainly from Asia, have Communist or Buddhist backgrounds and I've heard questions from them that I've never heard anyone ask before. Because of that, I've been driven into the Bible, not just out of mere intellectual curiosity, but because I *need* the information within to help the students with answers. Their eternal salvation is on the line so I want to have the verses to hand. And I want a fuller understanding of various subject matters so I'm not left stumped again in future. I can think back to several occasions when, having just finished an evening with the international students, all I've been able to think about is racing home to open my Bible because a question was raised that got my mind whirring and I've been desperate to know the answer.

While reading the Bible is an act of the will that sometimes requires self-discipline, you will find that as you apply what you're learning, you will increasingly come to the Bible out of desire, excitement or even sheer desperation rather than duty. Imagine if a soldier was being trained to use a weapon but was told he was never going to be sent into battle to use it. He could be quite half hearted about his training knowing it wouldn't make a huge difference to his life. But imagine a soldier is trained with a weapon and told he'll be going to the front line within two weeks. You can bet that soldier will be intensely focused on being the best that he can possibly be with it. The Bible is our spiritual "weapon" - the writer to the Hebrews calls it a sharp double-edged sword - and when we know we're going to be put to the front lines with it, we're going to focus more intensely in training ourselves with it.

Another area of sanctification that will accelerate through practical ministry is in regard to prayer. When we're getting ourselves into tight situations or confronting real spiritual enemies or attempting great things for God, we will find that our prayers are no longer full of empty rhetoric, trite platitudes or vain repetition. Instead, they will become passionate, pleading and authentic. The Bible records Peter being taken into prison for preaching the Gospel and it says, *"But while Peter was in prison, the church prayed very earnestly for him." (Acts 12:5)* The key word here is "earnestly". It means "with added intensity." Where did the intensity come from? Obviously because one of their number desperately needed God to come through for him. This wasn't some abstract or hypothetical prayer now. It was focused and full of intent. Similarly, you'll find through practical ministry that you become ready to wrestle with God in prayer for as long as it takes because, in faith, you've attempted great things beyond your human capabilities and you know that you'll fail unless he comes through for you. You'll become totally dependent on God and find you *need* His power. This is a scary but excellent situation to be in. When you come to the end of yourself you find the beginning of God and you'll find Him coming through for you in miraculous ways.

Similarly, when we're willing to go to the front lines and apply our training, our praise ceases to be mere ritualistic ceremony or hypocritical show. Like the 72 who returned from their mission brimming with joy, excitement and faith because they'd witnessed Jesus' power and glory with their own eyes, we will experience a similar thing in our own lives. When we come to sing before the Lord it will be real, raw, authentic, extravagant and spontaneous because we've just witnessed a hardened atheist find salvation. We've just seen a demon cast out. We've just seen someone healed. We've just seen prayers answered. No longer will God have reason to turn away from our worship, calling it hypocritical and false, as he did to Israel through Isaiah. Instead, our very lives will be like a sweet fragrance rising up to God (2 Cor 2:15) and our praise will be an overflow out of our joyful hearts.

And finally, when we're engaged in battle like this we will simply have no time for divisive idle gossip and priggish behaviour. We will have too much to be getting on with to be bothered with trivial arguments. When one of our number has just been arrested on hate speech charges for speaking against homosexuality in public, or proclaiming that there is no other way to heaven except but through Christ, and when we have to assemble to pray and petition for that man's freedom like the early church did for Peter, petty arguments about whether he was wearing a tie at the time of his arrest start to look ridiculous. When ten people have given their lives to the Lord because one of our number has been handing out Gospel tracts in public, the version of the Bible being used on them becomes of secondary importance. When one of our number has been asked a particularly tough question by an atheist that he couldn't answer and he brings it to the group to discuss because this man's salvation is at stake, arguments about the church sanctuary's lilies and tulips start to move down our list of priorities. We will become more attractive people to be around.

The reverse economy of God's kingdom means that the best way to improve ourselves is to try to help others. Through such things we'll learn to keep things in perspective. We'll learn humility. People will come to know the Lord Jesus through us. Our numbers will grow. Our faith will strengthen. We too, will turn from lambs into lions. We'll turn into the type of disciples who are ready to lay down our lives for Christ. We will find bonds of unity growing. We'll be one body. One Spirit. Authentic. Real. A band of brothers and sisters that need one another, with all our faults and frailties and idiosyncrasies, just to get by. This is what church should look like. And isn't this the kind of church everybody wants?

Chuck Swindoll said, *"In vain I have searched the Bible, looking for examples of early believers whose lives were marked by rigidity, predictability, inhibition, dullness, and caution. Fortunately, grim, frowning, joyless saints in Scriptures are conspicuous by their absence. Instead, the examples I find are of adventurous, risk-taking, enthusiastic, and authentic believers whose joy was contagious even in times of full trial. Their vision was broad even when death drew near. <u>Rules were few and changes were welcome.</u> The contrast between then and now is* *staggering."* I believe we can rediscover all that made the early church so winsome if we are willing to go out.

Indeed, there is nothing to lose by it and everything to gain.

# Chapter 7
# We Have Allowed The World To Become Cynical

*We are not called to escape the world. We are called to impact the world. We are called to transform the world. We are called to engage it. To change it. - Brian Burchik*

---

Cynicism is one of the most prominent hallmarks of our generation. People are more cynical now, about more things, than they've ever been. The individual reasons for it are varied but basically this disease, this cancer of the soul, is spread by one thing...disappointment.

As children we are idealistic and we freely put our hope and faith in others. It's our natural disposition to be open and trusting. If a parent tells a child that there's a Santa Claus or a tooth fairy, the child will believe them implicitly. If a man comes along offering sweets to a child, they don't perceive that the man might have ulterior motives. When I was a kid my sister offered me a white bar of soap in the shape of polar bear saying it was white chocolate as a practical joke. I took a bite without hesitation! Around the same age my dad offered me a bowl of fat saying it was jelly and I took a full spoon without even having a sniff. I had no reason not to trust them or believe everything I was told. Kids have a naivety, a trusting disposition, and an innocence about the true nature of the world.

As the child grows up however, they discover that almost all of this hope and trust is completely misplaced. Santa doesn't exist. Guys offering candy do have ulterior motives. People will constantly let you down. Give your heart to anything and it will be broken. Offer love and friendship and it'll be thrown back in your face. Try your hardest and you won't necessarily succeed. Life isn't often fair. People die. So will you. This growing realisation of disappointment begins to crush our souls and leads to teenage angst, depression, a hardening heart and cold cynicism. So great can this downtrodden feeling of hopelessness become that, for some, it even leads to thoughts of suicide. While most don't go to that extreme, the journey of childhood to adulthood is almost always a journey of idealism to cynicism. The more sin people encounter, the more disappointments and hurts they face and the more hardened and cynical they become about it all.

Now sin has become so rampant in the world today and we encounter it so often, that this generation currently nurses some of the most battered and bruised souls of all time. Consequently we have become one of the most cynical generations of all time. People today have come to believe that nothing is objective. Nothing is concrete. Nothing, and no-one, can be relied upon. There is nothing that you can hang your hat on. Nothing is real. The wizardry of Computer Generated Imagery (CGI) in movies and television has even taught us not to believe our own eyes. We've come to believe that everything is a fraud. Everything is a front. Everything is a fake. Look behind the surface of anything and you'll find it's always smoke and mirrors. In politics we have become so used to candidates promising us the earth on the campaign trail and then delivering nothing in office. We've become so used to hearing of them becoming embroiled in some scandal where they have lied, cheated or stolen behind our backs. Advertising companies make a business out of lying to us about products which promise health and satisfaction but which never deliver on that false hope. We know we are constantly being lied to in the media. We know that everyone is putting a spin on things, covering up truths, and that everyone is really out for what they can take from us. We start to believe that there's no-one with real integrity. Everyone can be bought for a price. Everyone is a hypocrite. Everyone is corrupt or corruptible. An epidemic of fatherless homes has taught us that we can't even trust our own blood relatives. People are becoming so jaded with it all. They're becoming tired of the constant hurt and disappointment. Often they can't even summon the strength to be angry anymore; they can only sigh and shrug in resignation. This is just...life. Might as well accept it. Many reach old age so world-weary that they're almost longing for the comfort of death. Cynicism, which is defined in the dictionary as "an attitude of scornful or jaded negativity, especially a general distrust of the integrity or professed motives of others" describes us in a nutshell. We have turned into the proverbial 'unbelieving generation'.

Now that same generation looks at the church and it sees no reason to believe we're any different.

They look at the scandals that have engulfed Catholicism - the corrupt cardinals and paedophile priests - and they falsely believe that the Vatican is representative of the Christian faith in some way. If you've seen *Know Your Enemy* you'll understand it isn't. It's just paganism in disguise.

They also turn on the television and see "Christian" channels filled with charlatan prosperity preachers sitting on ostentatious golden thrones, trying to milk money from their audience for private jets, or screaming into the microphone and performing Jedi mind tricks. If the lavish lifestyles these people lead are not repellent enough, very often it also won't be long before they're also found to be committing adultery, fraud or caught up in some homosexuality scandal where their ministry is exposed as a hollow sham.

Then there are the institutional churches - Episcopalian, Anglican, Church of Scotland etc. - who have become so liberal, theologically weak and desperate to bow to public pressure that they don't seem to really believe the Bible themselves anymore. In fact, they openly contradict it. Pressure came to allow female bishops and pastors and they capitulated. Pressure came to allow homosexual clergy and they capitulated again. Pressure then came to recognise homosexual marriage and they have capitulated once more. They're easily blown about with the opinion of the age and refuse to support the integrity of the Word of God. Within these churches you will therefore find, to varying degrees, acceptance of false religion, freemasonry, paganism (former Archbishop of Canterbury, Rowan Williams, was publicly installed as a Druid Priest at a pagan ceremony while still in office) as well as promotion of universalism, evolutionary theory and all kinds of other heretical teaching which significantly departs from the Bible. These churches take this liberal approach to attract people into their pews not realising that the message they're really giving the world is, *"look, this is all just a facade. This is all just a show. We don't even really believe this Book we preach from either. We're willing to ignore it or contradict if you want."* This simpering, flimsy, pandering, faithless faith is not only useless but it leaves the world asking the same questions as before: *"Is nothing real? Is nothing genuine? Is nothing authentic? If you don't even have the guts to stick with what you believe, why should we believe it either?"*

In other words, the most visible representatives of Christianity in the world today - the ones that unbelievers see most often - are often not Christians at all! The world looks at the corruption and deceit of these pagans, charlatans and apostates and it denigrates Jesus and his church because of them. Indeed, every time the world hears about a hypocrite who claims to represent Christianity, Jesus' name is dragged through the mud and people become more cynical and hardened towards the faith. (Rom 2:21-24)

Why isn't the true church reversing this opinion? Because the true church isn't visible!

## We Must Be Visible

Jesus told us, *"You are the light of the world—like a city on a hilltop that cannot be hidden. No one lights a lamp and then puts it under a basket. Instead, a lamp is placed on a stand, where it gives light to everyone in the house. In the same way, let your good deeds shine out for all to see, so that everyone will praise your heavenly Father." (Matthew 5:14-16)*

Jesus told us that we need to be visible in the world. Our good deeds need to shine out for everyone to see. Why? So that the world will see us and be inspired to praise God in heaven. If hypocrisy turns people away from God, integrity will turn people towards him. If evil deeds leads to distrust, good deeds will lead to trust. The world can only become cynical about the church when the church is hiding its light. We must be visible! More visible than paedophile priests, more visible that prosperity preachers and more visible than dead apostate institutions. We must become impossible to ignore. Indeed, we must reflect the vibrant, radiant glory of God Himself.

We must show the world that people of integrity do exist. In a world of style and no substance, we need to be a people full of substance. In a world of spin and deceit, we need to be a people of honesty. In a world of greed and corruption, we need to be a people of generosity and moral courage. In a world full of doubt and fear, we need to be a people of conviction. In a world full of hypocrisy, we need to be a people of the highest integrity. In a world full of takers we need to be givers. That's what people really need to see. They need to see that there is a God in whom we can trust and that it's a solid and unwavering hope. As God himself said, *"those who trust in me will not be disappointed." (Isa 49:23)* They need to see that through us.

Let them see that our lives are whole; that our lives are put together. Let them see that we have nothing to hide and nothing to fear. Let our lives be an open book. No spin necessary. Let us say to a watching world, *"go ahead and look. My behaviour will match my beliefs. My walk will match my talk. My character will match my confession."* People of integrity are not whitewashed tombs like the hypocritical Pharisees who looked good on the outside but who, inside, were full of impurity and who led people to blaspheme God. People of integrity are internally ordered and have a consistency in speech and action. They put excellence ahead of expedience, purity ahead of personal gain and righteousness ahead of riches. As we become visible in these things, we will start to reverse the world's cynicism and inspire people to worship, rather than blaspheme, our God in heaven.

Now there is a caveat to this - our good deeds should *never* be done to glorify ourselves and we must *never* boast about them. We must never tell people how much we're giving, how often we're praying or fasting or how many people we're saving. We must *never* blow our own trumpets. We must never look for position, titles, praise or rewards either. The only thing we're allowed to boast about is what Jesus has done for us. We can boast about that all we like! Indeed, we should shout about it from the rooftops! (Gal 6:14) Otherwise, just let your good deeds for others do the talking and give all glory to God. Also, remember that your motivation for doing a thing is more important than the act itself, so remain humble as you express the love of Christ to others.

*Bob Goff, founder of Restore International, says, "The media is always pegging Millennials for perpetually raising one eyebrow. "Cynicism is the hallmark of this generation," critics say, "and their enthusiasm is not easily earned." If this is true, what your generation needs is to stop being stingy—and start giving away your love and acceptance for free. Give your love away more extravagantly—more whimsically—in these coming years. Make it look like you're made of the stuff.*

*Extravagant love isn't satisfied just dangling its feet over the water in people's lives; it grabs its knees and does a cannonball. Grab your knees often—do it every day—and dive into people's lives in creative and winsome ways. If someone's having a lousy day, send them a pizza. Mail them a dozen baby ducks. Get a bread machine in your office, and just give warm bread to people—and give them real butter, not margarine.*

*In this reverse economy Jesus talks about, somehow the more inefficient we are with our love, the less it's wasted. There's something beautifully inefficient about just saying "Hello" and "How can I be helpful?" to people we don't know. People will know who we are and what we believe by how extravagant we are with our love."*

In a world of facade and fakery, the one thing this generation craves is something that's *real*. They want their cynicism to be proved wrong. They want someone to come along who won't let them down. They're dying for someone to show them something authentic. They're craving something that offers them genuine hope. Therefore, churches won't reach this generation by trying to manufacture a cool image; this world has seen enough images to know there's never much substance behind them. Churches will instead reach this generation by offering integrity, substance, truth and bucket loads of unconditional love. It's the only way to heal the soul cancer of cynicism that so many now live with. The Bible says that *"hope deferred makes the heart grow sick,"* (Proverbs 13:12). Well, hope demonstrated and delivered makes the heart grow strong. Let's demonstrate and deliver the sure hope we have in the Lord to a very sick world. Let's be the channel through which faith, hope and joy in Jesus Christ is rekindled.

## A Mindset Change

The fact that the world has become cynical about this closed up institution called the church is yet another reason why we need a mindset change in how we reach them. Although we're constantly trying to lure people into our building in comfortable and non-threatening ways, the more cynical people become about the church, the less likely they are to respond to that invitation. If they aren't put off "all organised religion" by the latest paedophile priest scandal in the news, their cynicism makes them distrustful of our motives. Their suspicion is that the only reason we want them there is to fill some pews and put some money in the collection basket. They think we're just part of some big fraud and they have no intention of playing along. So we have to take the initiative and go to them. Not asking anything from them but looking only for ways to serve them. This calls for cultural engagement outside of our four walls.

Imagine if we weren't just known for corrupt prosperity preachers who chase lavish lifestyles; imagine if we weren't known for Catholic priests who carry out pagan acts in the name of Christ; imagine if we weren't known for simpering, flimsy liberals who throw the Word of God out of the window every time they're challenged on it. Imagine if we were instead a community known for love of God; love of neighbours; defiantly speaking the truth; seeking the welfare of all the people; defying hatred and greed; feeding the hungry; clothing the naked; bearing each other's burdens; choosing self-sacrifice; voluntarily redistributing our resources for the benefit of all; amazing marriages; love of enemies; sexual purity; honesty; quick conflict resolution; devotion to God's Word; healings, signs and wonders and justice for the oppressed. Imagine if we were known to be people of such integrity that we are willing to be marginalised and even put to death rather than deny our King. Imagine the impact that would have on the world. In order to turn all these imaginings into reality, which is what we must do, we must start doing them and we must start being visible about doing them. Out there in the community. Just as Jesus commanded us to be. Christianity is not a private pursuit.

As we switch from a "come" culture back to a "go" culture, think about trying not to centre everything around your building. For example, instead of doing next year's nativity production in the sanctuary and telling people to invite their non-Christian friends, take it outside and perform it in the middle of your local mall where the people will already be. Instead of doing a tour of churches with your Christian band, do a tour of coffee houses. Instead of doing a bake sale in the church and trying to invite people in, bake a batch of goodies and then go into the community and give them away freely. You get the picture. Take the initiative to go to them.

Don't retreat into Christian ghettos online either. Instead of uploading your videos to GodTube, upload them to YouTube where unbelievers have a shot of finding them too. When you're posting about your faith on Facebook, don't set your filters so unbelieving friends can't see what you've written. Yes, some friends will argue with you about your faith and your friend count will drop, but you're going to impact some lives too. Just do something public. Be creative. Get out there. And always walk with integrity. A cynical world is going to be examining your behaviour for any signs of hypocrisy so let it always stand up to the scrutiny. As Paul wrote, *"Do everything without complaining and arguing so that no one can criticise* you. Live clean, innocent lives as children of God, shining like bright lights in a world full of crooked and perverse people." (Phil 2:15)

Listen to this story from a pastor who encountered a cynical taxi driver in New York City and you'll see the problem we face:

*"Years ago in New York City, I got into a taxi cab with an Iranian taxi driver, who could hardly speak English. I tried to explain to him where I wanted to go, and as he was pulling his car out of the parking place, he almost got hit by a van that on its side had a sign reading The _____ Church. He got real upset and said, "That guy's drunk." I said, "No, he's a Christian." He asked, "Do you know about church?" I said, "Well, I know a little bit about it; what do you know?"*

*It was a long trip from one end of Manhattan to the other, and all the way down he told me one horror story after another that he'd heard about the church. He knew about the pastor that ran off with the choir master's wife, the couple that had burned the church down and collected the insurance—every horrible thing you could imagine. We finally get to where we were going, I paid him, and as we're standing there on the landing I gave him an extra-large tip. He got a suspicious look in his eyes—he'd been around, you know.*

*I said, "Answer me this one question." Now keep in mind, I'm planning on witnessing to him. "If there was a God and he had a church, what would it be like?" He sat there for awhile making up his mind to play or not. Finally he sighed and said, "Well, if there was a God and he had a church—they would care for the poor, heal the sick, and they wouldn't charge you money to* teach you the Book." I turned around and it was like an explosion in my chest. "Oh, God." I just cried, I couldn't help it. I thought, "Oh Lord, they know. The world knows what it's supposed to be like. The only ones that don't know are the Church."

Now listen to this story and see what a difference loving acts can make. This one came out after Muslims started going on a murderous hunt for Christians in Egypt after a YouTube video criticising Mohammed went online.

"You've heard about this video that insults Mohammed and the protests haven't you? Well last week in Cairo a mob of 600 people armed with guns made their way to an Evangelical Church and painted a slogan on the wall saying, "Death to the worshipers of the cross!"

Praying inside was a church pastor with some 30 young people. They assumed the destruction of the building was inevitable but prayed for a miracle.

They damaged the downstairs bookshop. But then a man told the crowd to stop because Christians from that church had come to his aid and tended his wounds when he was hurt in the revolution. Another Muslim man told the crowd these were the Christians who had offered them water to wash with before their Muslim prayers. The crowd went silent, turned around and went on their way."

Source: Open Doors via HistoryMakers

Let's engage with the culture and put faith into action. It makes all the difference.

## Chapter 8
## We Lack The Spirit's Power

*"The Great Commission will never be accomplished by human effort or wise planning, though both are crucial for the task. We need God's power in order to carry the gospel into every part of the globe. Only God's power can transform rebels into disciples."*
*- Francis Chan*

---

I think the case has now been made that we need to "go". But like the disciples who were commanded to wait in the upper room for the Holy Spirit before they went, we must make sure that the Holy Spirit is powering our efforts too. How do we make sure of this?

In Stay Free we learned that internal change must always come before external change. We must become the right kind of tree before expecting the right kind of fruit. A good tree produces good fruit and a bad tree produces bad fruit.

Peter wrote, "*...Supplement your faith with a generous provision of moral excellence, and moral excellence with knowledge, and knowledge with self-control, and self-control with patient endurance, and patient endurance with godliness, and godliness with brotherly affection, and brotherly affection with love for everyone. The more you grow like this, the more productive and useful you will be in your knowledge of our Lord Jesus Christ.*" (2 Peter 1:5-8)

What Peter is saying here is that if you develop the right kind of inner character the right actions are naturally going to follow. As you grow in integrity and righteousness, you will automatically become productive for God's kingdom. Things you didn't even expect to happen will happen. Things you didn't even strive for are going to materialise. Doors will open. Things will change. And people will respond to it. They'll see something different in you. The right actions come almost as a by-product of attaining the right character.

In Stay Free we also learned that the only way we can become the right kind of person internally, the only way we can attain that right character, is to have the Holy Spirit in our hearts. Only He gives us the power to pursue such inner righteousness. The more we get into the habit of responding to Him in the right way, letting him overcome our own selfish desires, the more Christ-like we will become. This is sanctification. As our sanctification increases, the power of the Holy Spirit grows inside us and as it does so, the Spirit's power begins to be unleashed. It's for this reason that things automatically start to happen in our lives. Doors will open. Things we didn't aim for will come to us naturally. Our productivity for the Kingdom will increase. It all happens because the Holy Spirit is now working through us. It's not our strength or wisdom or knowledge; it's his. It is from his power inside us that Godly accomplishments automatically flow. It is from this Holy Spirit power inside us that we can do things well beyond our natural abilities. If we are to make the Holy Spirit the engine inside us that drives us forward, we must get into the habit of being obedient to Him so that His power is increasingly unfettered in our lives.

What I'm getting at is this: the Holy Spirit compels us towards righteousness and as we submit to him and become more righteous, the more the Holy Spirit can do through us.

**So the key to the power of the Holy Spirit is Righteousness.**

If we want to see the power of the Spirit, we must first seek righteousness. Let me explain how we gain righteousness using a very simple equation:

**Faith + Obedience = Righteousness  (F + O = R)**

Remember this. Since it is the key to unfettering the power of the Holy Spirit in our lives, it's worth taking the time to go through each of the components one-by-one.

## FAITH

*"He could not do any miracles there, except lay his hands on a few sick people and heal them. And he was amazed at their lack of faith."* (Mark 6:5-6)

The only recorded incident in the Bible where Jesus was restricted in the miracles he could perform, was when he arrived in a situation where there was no *faith*. Here Jesus had returned to his hometown - the place where he'd grown up as a child and worked as a carpenter for many years. You can imagine the kind of reception he got from the locals. *"That's not the Messiah! That's the guy who made my kitchen table!" "Him? Pffff! He was the boy that used to live down the street! He used to play with my kids! There's nothing special about him!"*

Because of their lack of faith that Jesus could perform miracles, he did not. What's extraordinary about this passage is that it says he *could* not. It's clear that if we want Jesus to move powerfully in our lives, we have to believe in his ability and willingness. Time and time again, Jesus performs miracles in response to faith.

*"Then he touched their eyes and said, "According to your **faith** will it be done to you"" (Matthew 9:29)*

*""Go," said Jesus, "your **faith** has healed you." Immediately he received his sight and followed Jesus along the road." (Mark 10:52)*

*"Then he said to her, "Daughter, your **faith** has healed you. Go in peace."" (Luke 8:48)*

*"Then he said to him, "Rise and go; your **faith** has made you well."" (Luke 17:19)*

*"He listened to Paul as he was speaking. Paul looked directly at him, saw that he had **faith** to be healed." (Acts 14:9)*

If we do not have faith that Jesus can and will, Jesus will not. There are many cessationists who don't believe Jesus can perform miracles today and because they don't believe it, they don't see it. Their lack of faith becomes a self-fulfilling prophecy. Contrary to Paul's command in 1 Thessalonians 5, they stifle the Spirit and so lose the Spirit's power. Yet Jesus says plainly that anyone who has faith him will do even greater things than those which he performed himself while on the Earth.

He says, *"Believe me when I say that I am in the Father and the Father is in me; or at least believe on the evidence of the miracles themselves. I tell you the truth, anyone who has **faith** in me will do what I have been doing. He will do even greater things than these, because I am going to the Father. And I will do whatever you ask in my name, so that the Son may bring glory to the Father. You may ask me for anything in my name, and I will do it." (John 14:11-14)*

No wonder the apostles were desperate for more!

*"The apostles said to the Lord, "Increase our **faith**!"" (Luke 17:5)*

We should always be looking, like the apostles, for more faith.

*"Then the disciples came to Jesus in private and asked, "Why couldn't we drive [the demon] out?" He replied, "Because you have so little **faith**. I tell you the truth, if you have **faith** as small as a mustard seed, you can say to this mountain, 'Move from here to there' and it will move. Nothing will be impossible for you."" (Matthew 17:19-20)*

In this verse the disciple's level of faith was not enough to drive a demon out of a possessed man. If they had more, they would have been able to. And then Jesus says something extraordinary. Faith can move mountains! In other words, by faith, there is literally nothing that is impossible according to God's will. The more faith we have, the more will we see God's power in our lives. In general we want to see things before we'll believe it. But God flips that around and says you have to believe it if you want to see it. For indeed faith is, *"the assurance of things hoped for and the conviction of things not seen."* (Heb 11:1)

## Obedience

Now here's the key which most people miss and which many people fight against: Faith always leads to obedient action. Faith that isn't supported by action, is no faith at all! James wrote, *"Dear brothers and sisters, what's the use of saying you have **faith** if you don't prove it by your **actions**? That kind of faith can't save anyone." (James 2:14)*

You may be surprised at the regularity with which the Bible couples the word 'faith/belief' with 'obedience/action'. The two are inextricably linked.

*"Later on God tested Abraham's **faith** and **obedience**. "Abraham!" God called. "Yes," he replied. "Here I am.""* (Genesis 22:1)

*"Through Christ, God has given us the privilege and authority to tell Gentiles everywhere what God has done for them, so that they will **believe** and **obey** him, bringing glory to his name."* (Romans 1:5)

*"But now as the prophets foretold and as the eternal God has commanded, this message is made known to all Gentiles everywhere, so that they might **believe** and **obey** Christ."* (Romans 16:26)

*"Jesus said to the people who **believed** in him, "You are truly my disciples if you keep **obeying** my teachings." (John 8:31)*

*"And all who **believe** in God's Son have eternal life. Those who don't **obey** the Son will never experience eternal life, but the wrath of God remains upon them.""* (John 3:36)

*"You see, he was trusting God so much that he was willing to do whatever God told him to do. His **faith** was made complete by what he did - by his **actions**."* (James 2:22)

As this book has been driving home, once Christians know about a truth they are obligated to apply it. Your faith is not complete unless you act on it. It's the tidal motion of discipleship. Indeed, *"As the body without the spirit is dead, so **faith** without **deeds** is dead."* (James 1:26)

So you see, faith and action are an inseparable pair. Faith comes by hearing and then once we have heard we must obey. If you don't have faith you won't act and if you don't act it's because you don't have true faith. True faith *always* shows. Indeed, professed faith that doesn't show in deeds is actually just hypocrisy. It's our deeds that bring integrity to our words. Our actions are always the real measure of what we believe.

*"A man's real belief is that which he lives by. What a man believes is the thing he does, not the thing he thinks."* - G MacDonald

An increase of faith always generates an increase in action; an increase in Godly action always generates an increase in faith. If we act on the small amount of faith we have now, like the 12 and 72 did, we'll see the reality of Jesus' words with our own eyes, which will give us more faith to try even bigger things in the future. What is more, and this is the key part of the equation right here, as we demonstrate our faith by obedience in this way, the Bible tells us that God considers us *righteous* in his sight. Faith + Obedience = Righteousness.

## RIGHTEOUSNESS

*"For we are **righteous** when we **obey** all the commands the LORD our God has given us.'" - (Deuteronomy 6:25)*

*"Zechariah and Elizabeth were **righteous** in God's eyes, careful to **obey** all of the Lord's commandments and regulations." (Luke 1:6)*

*"And a **righteous** person will **live by faith**." (Hebrews 10:38)*

*"And because of Abraham's **faith**, God declared him to be **righteous**." (Romans 4:22)*

The Bible isn't giving us a conflicting message when it tells us that *faith* leads to righteousness and then tells us that it's *obedience* that leads to righteousness. It's not teaching us works based salvation. It's just saying that faith and obedience are just two sides of the same coin. Because of their inseparable nature, the two can be used interchangeably. One implies the other. Only the faithful obey; only the obedient are truly faithful. When the Bible lists great examples of *faith* in Hebrews 11 it lists great *deeds*. And as James said when talking about Abraham, *"You see, his **faith** and his **actions** worked together. His **actions** made his **faith** complete." (James 2:22)*

So here it is again: **Faith + Obedience = Righteousness.**

And like we noted, this is the key to the power of the Holy Spirit being unfettered.

## POWER

The Bible gives us many benefits of righteousness.

It tells us that our prayers become powerful and effective. James writes, *"Confess your sins to each other and pray for each other so that you may be healed. The earnest prayer of a **righteous** person has great **power** and produces wonderful results." (James 5:16)*

It tells us that God will provide for our needs: *"Seek the Kingdom of God above all else, and live **righteously**, and he will give you everything you need." (Matthew 6:33)*

It tells us that God will strengthen us: *"The eyes of the LORD search the whole earth in order to strengthen those whose hearts are fully committed to him." (2 Chronicles 16:9)*

It also tells us that God will give us eternal life (Matt 25:46), we will be rewarded in heaven (2 Tim 4:8), God will walk with us (Gen 6:9), protect us (Gen 7:1), bless us (Prov 13:21), avenge us (Rev 6:10), we will become wiser (Prov 9:9), we will produce much good fruit which glorifies God (Philippians 1:11), we will be protected in battle with Satan (Eph 6:14). In fact, the simple faith in Christ which leads to righteousness is the key to everything! Both in this life and the next.

*"But we who live by the Spirit eagerly wait to receive by faith the **righteousness** God has promised to us." (Gal 5:5)*

If we truly want our prayers to be answered, if we truly want to see God moving powerfully in our lives, if we truly want to see a revival, if we want to see great things happening, if we want to emulate the early church and do even greater things than what we read about in the Bible as Jesus suggested, then we must be righteous. If we want good fruit, then we must first become the right kind of tree. Internal before external. We must become the right kind of people.

And this is the problem.

## Our Lack of Righteousness

We often don't really want to become the right kind of people.

You see, somewhere along the line the church decided that we could accept Jesus Christ as our Saviour but reject Him as our Lord. We decided that we could call ourselves followers of Christ without actually having to follow. We decided that all these things that Jesus tells us to do, we don't actually have to do them. We just have to memorise them. And study them. Or we have to learn them in Greek. The Bible says, *"Those who say they live in God should live their lives as Jesus did." (1 John 2:6)* but we look at that and somehow it doesn't register. Instead of being faithful we're fearful. Instead of being obedient we're rebellious. We don't really crave righteousness.

**We just crave the benefits of righteousness.**

We want our prayers to be powerful and effective, we want provision, his strength, blessings, protection, wisdom and power. We want the good things we read about in the Bible. The spectacular healings and miracles. The fulfilled prophecies. The revivals. We want those. We don't want what it takes to get those though. We don't want righteousness. We don't want to actually have to become like the kind of people the early apostles were, much less become like Jesus himself. We want their results; we don't want their character. We don't want to have to pick up our cross and follow Jesus along the narrow road. We don't really want to hand our lives over to the Holy Spirit and live a life of self-denial in faithful obedience to him. That's really...hard. We don't want it to cost us anything. Consequently, the church today is suffering from a real lack of righteousness. In fact, it's become really quite licentious.

You see, in our quest for comfort we have followed the world into hedonism. Churches today are filled with Christians who are living in adulterous relationships. They're full of people who are living together and sleeping together outside of marriage. It's full of people who regularly go to wild parties and abuse alcohol. Perhaps even abuse drugs. It's full of people who are chasing wealth and fame and the pleasures of the world. People who have no self-control to bridle their tongue and who let filth flow from their lips. People who are even involved in the occult - things like yoga, acupuncture or freemasonry. It's full of people who are wilfully disobeying the Word of God. Choosing to ignore God's commands. Not going public with their faith. Ignoring the Great Commission. Do we realise that cowardice is sin? Revelation 21:8 tells us so. *"But God has not given us a Spirit of fear and timidity but of power, love and self-discipline"* (2 Tim 1:7). For any number of these reasons, the church is full of *unrighteousness*.

Yet these very same people you will see on a Sunday morning shouting for revival, working themselves into a fervour, singing songs of worship and adoration, pleading for God to heal their sick, desperate for a sign or a miracle, craving a prophecy, vision or a word of knowledge. You will see them craving the power of the Spirit. "Then give up your adulterous relationship" God replies. "Hmmm...can't you give us all the miracles without us actually being obedient? Maybe if I just sing louder or tell you some more how much I love you...then the Spirit will come in power?"

It won't happen. The Bible tells us, *"The eyes of the Lord watch over those who do right, and his ears are open to their prayers. But the Lord turns his face against those who do evil."* (1 Peter 3:12) and *"We know that God doesn't listen to sinners, but he is ready to hear those who worship him and do his will."* (John 9:31)

We have to make a decision about the kind of people we want to be. Do we actually want to be like Jesus? If we aim for righteous character, we'll get the power thrown in. If we aim for the power, we'll get neither. *"God blesses those who hunger and thirst for righteousness, for they will be satisfied."* (Matthew 5:6)

## THE DANGER OF CRAVING POWER WITHOUT RIGHTEOUSNESS

Craving power and blessing without being willing to pick up our cross and pursue righteousness is futile, but it's also dangerous. Because in that situation our focus is becoming misplaced - it's now on the gifts rather than the Giver of the gifts. It's on supernatural experiences rather than God Himself. What we're really saying to God is, *"no, we don't want to actually have to follow you. We just want what you can give us. We don't want to develop a relationship with you. Just give us the goodies and don't ask anything of us."* We're starting to treat God like a genie again - a cosmic butler who is there to lavish us with gifts and sweep up after the mess we make while pursuing a reckless lifestyle. We're starting to become self-centred rather than God centred. Imagine a child who didn't want a relationship with his parents but constantly demanded and expected gifts from them. Imagine a child who ignored all his parent's instruction but who still demanded to be bailed out of trouble every time they landed in prison. That child would be regarded as a self-centred brat, and rightly so. But this is a picture of the Western church so very often.

What you'll see in many churches today is an evil and adulterous generation who are constantly demanding miraculous signs but who have no intention of being faithful or obedient. They feel that God needs to come into our church services to prove himself, to entertain us, to wow us, to make our church performances more spectacular. If we're sick he should heal some people and do supernatural things. We don't mind what he does, as long as it's spiritual and makes us feel warm and fuzzy. If people bark like dogs, wriggle like snakes, shake or laugh uncontrollably or fall over, that's all good. We don't care. We just want something supernatural. And when the show is over we want him to leave us alone so that we can go back to our own sinful lives. Back to sleeping with our unmarried partner. Back to those drunken parties. Back to swearing like a trooper.

## The Flesh

Now when God doesn't respond to our demands by moving in power and that is the thing we're most focused on and most desperate for, we can often find ourselves slipping into the 'flesh' instead. That is, trying to do things in our own strength to compensate for the lack of genuine Holy Spirit power. AW Tozer wrote, *"I say that a Christian congregation can survive and often appear to prosper in the community by the exercise of human talent and without any touch from the Holy Spirit! All that religious activity and the dear people will not know anything better until the great and terrible day when our self-employed talents are burned with fire and only that which was wrought by the Holy Ghost will stand forever!"*

"The Flesh" is basically an attempt to fill the gap that the Holy Spirit should occupy by our own efforts. It's characterised by strong self-delusion and wishful thinking. In fleshly churches you'll hear people constantly prophesying that a great new move of God is just around the corner and yet it never comes. People will go with it because it tickles their ears and it's what they want to hear. And so they just bounce from one vague vision or prophecy to the next. Revival, outpouring and blessing is always promised to be just ahead in these churches. It's the tomorrow that never comes. There have also been famous examples of false prophets trying to set dates for Jesus' second coming, despite his explicit warnings not to. When the date comes and goes without incident, the false prophets just re-calibrate and try again. In fleshly churches, the real speaking of tongues is replaced with gibberish. It turns into "I-untie-my-bow-tie" and "I-came-in-a-Honda" type stuff (say those repeatedly really fast and you'll see what I mean). Cheap parlour tricks replace real miracles. There was a craze a few years ago where every 'faith healer' worth his salt was doing the leg-lengthening trick to wow audiences. He would get a participant to sit in a chair with their legs extended. One of their legs would be shorter than the other, and then through a little bit of physical, emotional and mental manipulation, the shorter leg would appear to grow out until it was of equal length. The flesh is what we would *like* to see happen and so it can lead to real self-delusion. What is worse however, is that when we're this desperate to see power and it doesn't come from God, we can even turn to demonic substitutes instead.

## The Demonic

Satan has power. His demons have power. Power enough to wow your average human being. You may have seen people in pagan cultures who are able to pierce themselves without bleeding or perform acts of superhuman strength. It's demonic power. So when we're desperate to see demonstrations of power without being willing to pursue righteousness, sometimes, if it suits the enemy's agenda, demons will fill the void and perform super-human feats like those seen in pagan cultures. Revelation 16:14 refers to demons who are able to do miracles for the purpose of deception. Because miracles are what we want to see, we'll do anything to convince ourselves that what we are witnessing is from God. Therefore you get people going into uncontrollable spasms, shaking, gold dust, orbs, angels of light, animal behaviours and any number of supernatural phenomena. All of it is given a Christian spin in an attempt to convince ourselves that it's really from God.

I spent most of my teenage years in a Pentecostal church and this is all very vivid to me. I remember going to Canada when the "Toronto Blessing" was all kicking off in the mid 90s and witnessed it first hand. Someone started crowing like a cockerel and the man on the stage announced that this was God heralding the dawn of a new age! Everybody cheered. Someone else starting barking and running around on all fours like a dog. The man on the stage interpreted this as God saying he was guarding the church from Satanic attacks! Everybody cheered. Of course the irony is that all of those things are precisely demonic. It was merely being ascribed to the Holy Spirit because everyone desperately wanted it to be from the Holy Spirit. People were just desperate for supernatural signs. Demons ended up running rampant in the church because people were focused on power, gifts, signs and wonders rather than faithful obedience and righteousness.

People forget Jesus command: *"Seek the Kingdom of God above all else, and live righteously, and he will give you everything you need." (Matt 6:33)* We must seek God and righteousness *above all else.* Should we need supernatural intervention from God as we seek those things, He will provide it according to His will. But those things should not be our ultimate focus.

One thing I've tried to hammer home through each Fuel Project series is that Satanism is very egocentric or self-centred. So you'll find the theology in the churches where demons are running rampant becomes very egocentric. The Holy Spirit almost starts being referred to as a drug from which you can get a 'spiritual high'. He'll give you the giggles or make you feel light-headed or behave like you're drunk. When hands are laid on for prayer they always go along the lines of "fill him up, give him more, right up to the top, more, more, more." It's all about trying to get a buzz off the Spirit. In fact, I remember during the Toronto Blessing people boasting that they didn't need drugs because they got a "spiritual high" from the Holy Spirit. They were quite open about it. At the extreme end of this you have people like John Crowder, who talks about "toking the ghost" and acting drunk on stage, as well as others like Todd Bentley.

At the root of it all is the idea that we want healing; we want supernatural phenomena; we want gifts. We want, we want, we want. The bottom line is we want to feel good without actually having to be good. We want the power without the righteousness. And when the supernatural is what we want above all else, we'll be more than willing to throw discernment out the window and accept demonic counterfeits.

## Why Does God Let This Happen?

Why would God let demons respond when people are praying to Him? The answers come through a couple of Bible passages. The first is from the prophet Ezekiel:

*"Then some of the leaders of Israel visited me, and while they were sitting with me, this message came to me from the LORD: "Son of man, these leaders have set up idols in their hearts. They have embraced things that will make them fall into sin. Why should I listen to their requests? Tell them, 'This is what the Sovereign LORD says: The people of Israel have set up idols in their hearts and fallen into sin, and then they go to a prophet asking for a message. So I, the LORD, will give them the kind of answer their great idolatry deserves." (Ezekiel 14:1-4)*

Other versions of the Bible translate it as, *"I will answer them myself in keeping with their idolatry"* or *"I will answer them according to their idols."* The people had idols in their heart meaning they wanted something more than they wanted God himself. And so God answered them according to their idols, which basically means he gave them the answers they wanted, as a kind of punishment. Remember when Pharaoh hardened his heart and wouldn't let Israel go so God hardened it further? It's a similar idea.

Another verse gives insight into this from the New Testament. Paul is talking about the Antichrist when he says:

*"This man will come to do the work of Satan with counterfeit power and signs and miracles. He will use every kind of evil deception to fool those on their way to destruction, because they refuse to love and accept the truth that would save them. So God will cause them to be greatly deceived, and they will believe these lies." (2 Thess 2:9-11)*

Again we see this idea that God is willing to send a delusion so that people get the idols they want in their hearts. If we ignore what God has told us to do then he is rightly offended that we have not loved or accepted the truth and we will instead get the deception we crave. If we want signs and wonders and power without wanting God himself, we'll get signs and wonders of a demonic nature. It's through such lack of discernment that many will receive the Antichrist himself. Our focus therefore should never be on the miracles but always on God himself and on righteousness. We must concentrate on living in faithful obedience knowing that the signs and wonders will follow those that believe.

2 Corinthians 11:4 says, *"You happily put up with whatever anyone tells you, even if they preach a different Jesus than the one we preach, or a different kind of Spirit than the one you received, or a different kind of gospel than the one you believed."* People can preach a Jesus that isn't the Jesus of the Bible. They can receive a Spirit that's different from the Holy Spirit of the Bible. They can preach a gospel that's different from the one in the Bible. They can preach and receive demonic counterfeits. We must be discerning at all times.

## Cessationism?

Now all the cessationists who believe that supernatural signs and wonders finished with the apostles might be standing and cheering at this point. But remember that Satan sends errors into the world in pairs of opposites and in its own way cessationism is just as bad. Because if the fleshly and demonic nonsense of the charismatic movement has made you cynical about the Spirit and blocked off your mind to the idea that He is alive and well and able to move in power today, then the enemy has won a victory over you too. Tozer rightly said, *"Anything that God has ever done, He can do now. Anything that God has done anywhere else, He can do here. Anything that God has done for anyone else, He can do for you."*

Not only is lack of faith in miracles a self-fulfilling prophecy that quenches the power of the Spirit, but Christians who avoid the Holy Spirit or the very idea of things pertaining to spiritual matters tend to become spiritually dull. So spiritually dull that many are in fact, still involved with demons without even knowing it.

For example, there are many Freemasons in the church who are unaware that they are part of a Satanic organisation. There are church-goers who don't believe God can still heal today, yet they will turn to Reiki healers or acupuncturists for their aches and pains. In fact, at my own church there is a man who does acupuncture for a living. When I asked him how much business he gets from church he replied that they account for over half his income! It's tragic. Acupuncture is predicated on Taoist philosophies - an offshoot of Buddhism. Doctrines of demons. Christians who live without reference to the supernatural become so spiritually dull that they don't see the danger in it or even give credence to the fact that they're opening themselves up to demonic entities. Shockingly, it is reported that some 40% of American Christians don't even believe Satan exists. Because of this lack of spiritual awareness, we have self-proclaimed Christians whose theology says that that Jesus can't heal them but who have no problem believing that Buddhist philosophies can. How tragic.

Many get involved with occult healing it because "it works!" It may well work. But there will always be a price to pay for it in the end. Demons do have the power to do miracles and if it keeps you deceived and enslaved to the occult practice it's in their best interests to make it work - at least superficially or in the short term. But don't be surprised if you soon start battling with depression, night-terrors, fears or other illnesses which just so happen to come along the moment you open yourself up to acupuncture or something like it.

Similarly, many Christians have now taken up yoga, which is nothing but Hinduism. They read horoscopes 'because it's just a bit of fun'. When they go on holiday and visit pagan temples they will submit to demands to take off their shoes - an act which signifies that they are walking on holy ground - giving respect and honour to demonic gods. Likewise, women will cover their heads as these gods require. Perhaps they'll even eat the food offered to the idols. I recently heard of a pastor who was offered some of this food from a Hindu temple and he ate it so as not to offend his hosts. Seemingly he was more concerned about not causing offence to people than he was to God. GK Chesterton rightly wrote that *"we fear men so much because we fear God so little."* It needs to be the other way around. The worst thing is that when this pastor told the story in church, the congregation found the whole situation hilarious. When honouring demons is met with laughter in church, we are dealing with extreme spiritual dullness.

You'll see Christians wearing lucky charm bracelets, attending hypnosis shows, joining martial arts classes or playing with ouija boards and other fortune telling devices. The church is full of this unrighteousness. It is incredible that it should be this way and that often, Christians are so spiritually dull that they don't see any conflict with these things and their faith in Jesus. This lack of spiritual awareness tends to always come from cessationists who have shut off their minds to the reality of spiritual power - both good and bad.

Why are we looking for healing from Taoist acupuncture when God offers healing? Why are we looking for protection from lucky charms when God offers us protection? Why are we looking for demons to tell us the future when God has given us prophecy in His Word and tells us to trust Him for provision? Why are we looking for demons to do for us what God has promised He would do for us? Because supernatural signs and wonders from demons doesn't cost us anything. It's a shortcut. Demons don't require us to put away our sin and be righteous by faithful obedience. It's *easier* and it suits our desire for comfort.

## Revival

Before we finish this chapter I need to say something about revival. Revival is one of those words you hear a lot in churches. Christians are constantly praying for revival. "Lord, send revival! We need revival!" Now frankly I don't think many of us really know what we're praying for when we use this word. And I have a feeling the image we each have in our heads would be different from person-to-person. But there's just a general feeling that we all want it.

However, if the picture you have in your head of revival is the one that has been planted there by televangelists, one of large church meetings where people are shaking, falling down, barking like dogs, having epileptic fits on the floor and laughing uncontrollably - basically an extra entertaining and spectacular church show that requires nothing from you - you may get what you wish for but be sure that it isn't revival. It's Satanic. It won't have any lasting benefit.

Look throughout history and you'll discover that true revival is always preceded by a sudden deep awareness of sin and an outpouring of heartfelt repentance for unrighteousness. All true revivals are marked by this overpowering desire to turn away from sin and towards righteousness and faithful obedience to the Word of God. That must come first. Until we are willing to see our sin for what it is, repent of it and pursue righteousness with an uncommon desperation, we will not see the power of God that we desire and we will instead be forever caught up in cheap imitations from humans or demons.

*"Have you noticed how much praying for revival has been going on of late - and how little revival has resulted? I believe the problem is that we have been trying to substitute praying for obeying, and it simply will not work." - AW Tozer*

*"You will rarely see what God is willing to do in secret until He sees what you are willing to do in public." - Tony Evans*

# Chapter 9
## We Love Our Traditions Too Much

*"A joke is a very serious thing." – Winston Churchill*

---

Recently someone posted a video on the Fuel Project Facebook page of a Christian comedian called Tim Hawkins. Hawkins was pointing out the absurdities of our church traditions and as with all observational humour, the laughter from the congregation came through the recognition that what he was saying was actually true. You can watch the video here: http://www.youtube.com/watch?v=mva4_xhFLVI.

I've seen a few Christian stand-up comedians or church groups doing skits on YouTube that highlight and poke fun at the habits, rituals or language of the church like this (Here is another http://www.youtube.com/watch?v=pzqaITA3IO0). And what all these videos are basically doing is holding a mirror up to ourselves and saying, "isn't it ridiculous that we do that?" Or "don't we all hate that part of church?" Or "isn't that thing we do completely fake?" Church satirists are like the child in "The Emperor's New Clothes". The one who dares to shout out from the crowd what everyone is thinking but would never say out loud. The one that dares to point out how ridiculous we all look. Satire strips away the facade and cuts through the posturing, the pretence and pomposity to expose truths that we all know deep down. That's why we can relate to it and what makes it funny. As it has often been said, *"there's many a true word spoken in jest."*

But once the laughter stops, there are serious questions that must naturally follow.

Like, "why do we continue with those habits if we really know deep down they're ridiculous? Why do we follow these traditions when we don't like them? If that thing we do is fake, and deep down we all know it, then why do we keep doing it? Once the mask has slipped and we've seen ourselves for what we are, can't we just take the mask off altogether and drop the act now? Isn't it time to get real with one another?"

For example, Tim Hawkins joked about how we all hate it when the pastor asks us to get up and shake hands with the people around us. And it's true. And that's why the audience were cracking up. But doesn't it make a mockery of the idea that we're a close fellowship, a band of brothers, a new community in Christ, when we actually really hate having to even say hello to the person beside us? He also joked about how bored we can get during worship time and how our legs get sore from standing up so long and how we start thinking about the other places that we have to be. And that can be true as well. But when we're all getting restless and bored and start looking at our watches during 'worship-time', doesn't that reveal that we're not actually worshipping at all and that something has gone wrong there? Shouldn't we be addressing the problem instead of carrying on with the same old worship model week-after-week? When satire highlights that much of what we do is just empty tradition and dead ritual and deep down everyone knows it is, why do we continue with it? Why do our church services still follow these patterns?

As we've already explored, one of the reasons that we coop ourselves up and go through these rituals is because, although it can be boring, it's easier than going out and practically loving our neighbours as ourselves. Passive ritual is always easier than authentic love. Authentic love involves risk. But another reason our services follow these patterns is because we simply cannot conceive of church as being any other way. If we weren't to go through these motions, we really wouldn't know what else to do. We wouldn't know what church was supposed to look like.

You see, when we think of Christianity there are certain images which instantly form in our minds. Christianity is (depending on your church background, or lack of it) spires, pews, dog collars, robes, pipe organs, denominations, old ladies with hats, membership classes, dusty hymn books containing tunes no newer than 200 years of age, archaic language full of thees and thous and other such things. You'll have your own mental images I'm sure. Perhaps the main preconception of church that will be common to everyone, is the service format. Almost everyone believes that church is Sunday morning, 11am or thereabouts, starting with a welcome time, then worship, then collection and announcements, then the sermon monologue, then a closing song, then tea and coffee, and then home. This service ritual literally *is* church to many.

Very few of us have ever stopped to ask the question, "where did these images come from? Where did these routines and formulas come from? Are they in the Bible? Are they actually achieving anything? Are they beneficial? Is this what Jesus intended?"

The truth is that none of those things I just mentioned, and a whole lot more of what we call Christianity today, is in the Bible at all. They are simply traditions that we have inherited from our parents, who in turn, inherited it from theirs. And as the baton is being passed down the generations, no one ever stops to think, "where did this begin?" or "why are we still doing this?" It's vitally important we keep asking these kinds of questions. Because when we *don't* continually ask these questions, it opens the door for man-made habits and institutional traditions of church life to gradually accumulate and exert more of an influence on the minds of the people than the Bible itself. If we allow that to happen we'll eventually be practicing something completely different from what Jesus intended, without realising it.

The most terrible example of this phenomenon is of course, the Roman Catholic church. About two thousand years ago the Christian message entered into Rome in a pure form but as the years rolled by, pagan traditions and superstitions began blending with it and polluting it. For a thousand years these traditions accumulated and were handed down through the generations with nobody stopping to question whether what they were practicing still looked anything like Jesus intended. Eventually they ended up with something so far from the truth that it was nothing but dead, cold, lifeless paganism with only a superficial facade of Christianity. Why did nobody take a moment to refer to the Bible throughout these thousand years to see how far off track they had gone? The simple answer is that they couldn't. The increasingly corrupt Catholic leaders didn't want the ordinary people to know that it had ceased to look anything like New Testament Christianity because they were profiting from the whole thing. So they deliberately restricted the availability of the Bible to Latin, which was a language that nobody could read except the professional clergy, and this created a dependency on the Catholic priests and institution. Since the average person couldn't refer to the Bible themselves they simply had to accept and trust that what they were being told was true. The priests took advantage of their power by spouting self-serving lies and of course, as they grew wealthier and exerted more influence over the people, the corruption continued and grew unabated. The ordinary person reached a point where they couldn't conceive that church could look any other way. To them, the Roman Catholic system *was* church. They couldn't see that this was nothing like Jesus intended. Their image of church was formed entirely by tradition and culture; not by the Bible. This period of ignorance became known as the Dark Ages. And it wasn't until the Reformers came along and started pulling these corrupt traditions down that Christianity began to move back in the right direction.

However, to use a *Stay Free* metaphor, the Reformers only moved things from a midnight sky to a 4am sky. They didn't bring things all the way through to midday. In other words, although the Reformers improved things by bringing *some* light into the Dark Ages, they didn't return the church to a truly original, Biblical condition. Not by a long shot. They retained much pollution from the culture in which they lived. For example, Martin Luther retained the Catholic idea of transubstantiation. That's nowhere to be found in the Bible. Plus he retained the idea of infant baptism. He retained the anti-Semitism of the Catholic church. These are just a few pollutants from Catholicism that weren't quite purged. The behaviour of the Reformers was sometimes quite "Catholic" too in the sense they could deal violently with dissenters. They were still a product of their Catholic culture in some ways. Don't get me wrong, Martin Luther and the other Reformers deserve a great deal of credit for moving things in the right direction in the face of much persecution but they didn't quite manage to purge all of the pollution and man-made tradition from the faith. And in many ways we're still in the same position as they were and in need of another Reformation - another round of tradition dismantling - to bring us all the way back to the midday sky of original Christianity. Many of our ideas of what church looks like goes back to the Reformation era (if not the Catholic Dark Ages) and even since then, Christianity has re-accumulated debris and pollution in the past 500 years that few people ever really stop to question. The traditions now have become so engrained that we find it hard to differentiate between what is man-made and what is truly Biblical. There's really no reason why this should be so. Unlike the Dark Ages, we *do* have personal access to the scriptures. Our Biblical illiteracy cannot be blamed on a lack of availability. It's very important we study the Word and continually compare our habits with the New Testament example.

## Churchianity

The modern term for a Christian faith system which places more emphasis on man-made habits and institutional traditions than the Bible is *"Churchianity"*.

Here are a couple of examples of Churchianity.

For a long while, and even until now, there was the notion that all worship music in churches had to be played on a lone pipe organ. Are pipe organs mentioned in the Bible? Nope. Is it a particularly holy instrument? Nope. Is it God's favoured brand of music? Nope. So why do some churches insist that it's the only valid instrument for worship? Simply because of people clinging to a tradition that began a few hundred years ago.

Why are "dog collars" associated with Christian ministers? Are they mentioned in the Bible? Nope. Not even a little bit? Nope. Well, where did that come from? The simple reason is that at one point it was fashionable for all men to wear them but as trends changed and society moved on, the conservative clergy refused to give up the look and clung to them. And thus they became a tradition. Really, dog collars no more Christian than powdered wigs or Cavalier hats.

A lot of dead tradition actually didn't start off as anything bad. Much of it actually started off as an authentic act by someone, somewhere. When pipe organs developed into what we know them as today, around the 17th century, they were such fantastically impressive instruments that made such a great noise, that of course people were excited to hear what it would sound like to get these things into their churches. At that time pipe organs were the most complex piece of machinery that man had ever engineered and it was a prestige instrument. People were excited by them and wanted to worship God on the best thing they had going. It was an authentic act. Why not get these musical wonders installed in churches and see what kind of noise they can make? However, as time wore on and musical tastes and fashions changed, it was conservative legalism, religiosity and Churchianity that meant churches stayed rooted in the past. An idol was made of the pipe organ and as new instruments threatened to make their way into church they were decried as 'worldly'. There is of course, no such thing as a worldly instrument or a holy instrument. All instruments are morally neutral and suitable for praising God (Psalm 150). So one generation's authentic act became the succeeding generation's idolatrous stale tradition.

There's a great example of this phenomenon in the Bible that will help explain what I mean. You may remember in the Old Testament how God instructed Moses to set up a bronze serpent on a stick, so that whoever looked at it would be healed of their snake bite in the desert. That was initially an authentic act. However, later in the Bible we're told that King Hezekiah had to destroy that very same bronze serpent because the Israelites had made an idol out of it in their minds and had started to worship it! Thus, what was once good and which served an important purpose now needed to be destroyed.

This is what happens in church. Not all tradition was outright pollution from the start. Often one generation's authentic act just gets inherited by following generations and as the baton is passed down it becomes stale, archaic, empty and even idolatrous tradition. And isn't that how much of the modern world sees the church? Stale? Archaic? Full of irrelevant tradition? What the world is looking at to form that opinion isn't authentic, Biblical Christianity. It's our Churchianity. It's our tradition and ritual. It's our pipe organs, pews, indecipherable hymns, insistence on using 17th Century English and strange clothing. Things which have no root in the Bible itself but which have accumulated over the years. Therefore, people are often not rejecting Jesus because of Jesus; they're rejecting Jesus because of us! We're not representing our Saviour to the world; we're representing our idolatrous institution to the world. It's those institutional traditions and rituals, the cold legalism and irrelevance, that often act as the barrier between people and Christ.

We must be careful not to get in the way. The lost soul doesn't need your version of the Bible, your dress code, your denomination or your legalism. They just need Jesus. It's important that we strip back all the debris and pollution and get back to authentic, real faith, as presented in the New Testament and learn how to communicate that to others. We do this primarily through authentic, spontaneous, extravagant acts of love...of which sharing the Gospel is the most powerful expression.

If your experience of church is a two-tiered system of members and non-members and you are not allowed to serve or use the church parking spaces nearest to the door until you sign your name on a register, your experience was with Churchianity. If you've ever been rejected or been made to feel an outsider because you didn't dress the right way or didn't have the right Christianese jargon to fit in, you were dealing with Churchianity. If fellowship means attending services with "our own race/social/economic/denominational kind" only and contact with those from the wider body of Christ is discouraged or seen as disloyal, you're dealing with Churchianity. If you have ever heard someone describe guitars or drums as ungodly, you were dealing with Churchianity. If your church places emphasis on legalistic rules and regulations created by the pastoral team or eldership without Biblical foundation, it's Churchianity. Churchianity is simply rife in the world today. We love our own traditions too much.

In fact, I read an interesting quote on Facebook from a Baptist minister called Andrew Fuller recently. He said, *"If we wish to see the Baptist denomination prosper, we must not expend our zeal so much in endeavouring to make men Baptists, as in labouring to make Baptists and others Christians."* Underneath, there was the comment from another Baptist minister who hadn't quite grasped the message: *"As a Reformed Baptist I must say a hearty AMEN to this quote from Mr. Fuller. Once someone is converted we have plenty of time to bring them to our church traditions..."*

Do you see the mindset? The idea that once someone is converted, the next phase is to start intentionally burdening them with our irrelevant, stuffy, archaic traditions and specific brand of Churchianity is ludicrous but all too common. To be honest, it doesn't matter one jot whether the Baptist denomination prospers. It doesn't matter that *any* denomination prospers! Denominations are one of those ideas you won't find in the New Testament. What matters is that people are finding Christ, being transformed by Christ, transforming others for Christ, and living their lives in faithful obedience to Christ. If that's happening, our man-made systems just don't matter.

And how many people have been put off Christianity because of this attitude? How many people have come looking for Jesus, enthused by the message of the Gospel, hearing this inspiring message of liberty and hope, seeing his relevance and glory, and then are confused and repelled when they are directed to a church to find that it is full of vain repetition, archaic tradition, dead language, old routines and rituals practiced by cold, judgmental people? Christ is *so* relevant and our traditions are very often so irrelevant. If people are to reject Christianity, let it be because they have honestly rejected the person of Christ and not because they are put off by our churchy traditions. Mahatma Ghandi famously said, *"I like your Christ but I do not like your Christians. They are so unlike your Christ."* What he was looking at were people who were letting their Churchianity get in the way of Jesus.

There is no reason why people shouldn't sing to God with every instrument imaginable. There's no reason why we shouldn't sing songs written last week as well as ones written last century. Or why we shouldn't be sitting in chairs instead of pews. Or why the minister shouldn't be wearing anything he wants within the boundaries of taste and decency. Or why the message of God should be shrouded behind language few people today fully grasp. And why we shouldn't accept anyone into the church, whatever they look like or however much money they have...or don't have.

Churchanity is just another undesirable consequence of the move from an organic to organisational form of Christianity. As we moved from the Chinese model to the Russian model, we became dependent on institutions and professional clergy and their traditions were part of the deal. Now if those things were to be taken away, we wouldn't know what to do with ourselves. But I want us to start thinking along those lines. If all we had to inform us was the Bible, what kind of church would we end up with? What kind of church would we be? We need to dismantle the traditions and the dependency on the institutions that created them to get back to the authentic, empowering faith that we read about in the New Testament.

## Change Rarely Comes From The Top

The problem is that once an organisation or institution is set in its ways, it will very rarely, if ever, dismantle its own traditions. Institutions are naturally conservative because of a deeply held desire to survive. And normally always the people at the top of the institutions are benefiting from the current arrangement too much to want to change it. The Catholic church had no intention of changing its ways prior to the Reformation because too many priests were benefiting from what they had and the status quo suited them. It took a radical group of reformers to expose the old corruption and begin again. True change always tends to come in such ways. From small groups of idealistic, radical believers who are not encumbered with the comfort, safety, wealth or power of the organisation and who therefore have nothing to lose. They are simply driven by doing the right thing. It's that purity of vision and motivation that often makes the difference. Earlier in this book I suggested that pastors scrap the Sunday morning ritual one morning, close the doors and tell their congregation that they were all going to hit the streets and make a difference in the community instead - even at the expense of losing members or facing a backlash. Unfortunately, I find it hard to envision pastors making such demands of their church because of the potential fallout. As I said, it pays institutions to be conservative and comfortable rather than radical.

Joel Arthur Barker said, *"New paradigms put everyone practicing the old paradigm at risk. The higher one's position, the greater the risk. The better you are at your paradigm, the more you have invested in it, the more you have to lose by changing the paradigms."* That's often where the resistance comes from.

You may remember a scene from Braveheart where Robert the Bruce is talking with his father about joining William Wallace's quest for freedom. The young Bruce is inspired by Wallace's idealism and passion. *"This Wallace...he doesn't even have a knighthood. But he fights with passion and he inspires!"* Bruce's diseased father laughs mockingly and replies, *"And you wish to charge off and fight as he did, eh?"* The Bruce nods his head: *"Maybe it's time...."* The old man stops laughing abruptly and makes his point clear: *"It is time to <u>survive</u>. You're the seventeenth Robert Bruce. The sixteen before you passed you land and title because they didn't charge in. Call a meeting of the nobles."* The younger Bruce doesn't like the idea at all: *"They do nothing but talk."* Bruce's father interjects: *"Rightly so. They're as rich in English titles as they are in Scottish, just as we are. You admire this man, this William Wallace. Uncompromising men are easy to admire. He has courage; so does a dog. But it is exactly the ability to compromise that makes a man noble."*

The Bruce's father wants to preserve the status quo - he wants to keep the wealth, the land, the titles, the prestige - and so he calls for cowardice and compromise. It tends to always be this way. Change doesn't generally come from those at the top who have much to lose by the abolition of the old system.

Notice how political candidates are full of honesty and vigour prior to elections when they have nothing to lose. Then once they are in office and have the power, all their idealism goes out the window. Now they have too much to lose. Suddenly you can't get an honest answer out of them in an interview and they would rather compromise and do dirty deals behind the scenes to hold onto their position than take uncompromising, self-sacrificial action. As soon as they are voted out and have nothing to lose again, they start coming clean; publishing memoirs that lift the lid on what really went on behind the scenes. This same kind of phenomenon can even exist within the church.

Real change rarely comes from within the established structures but rather comes from a radical group of uncompromising of believers who come together with a clarity of vision, purpose and courage. People who are simply willing to look at the Bible and say, "forget the traditions, forget the clichéd images, the current paradigm, the way things have always been, forget who wins or loses by this...what does the Bible *actually* say? Let's do that."

The church is in need of a reset. And for that reset, we need to look well beyond the 4am skies of the Reformation for our inspiration and look to the bright and shining noonday sun of the early church itself. Not only does the church need this, but the world needs it too.

# Chapter 10
## We Don't Get Answers In Church

When I was at school I was never very interested in German class. I had to do it because it was part of the curriculum but I had no plans to live in Germany or to work there. It wasn't even a place I expected to visit. And even if I did happen to briefly pass through their borders, I expected that Germans would be able to speak English and therefore, communication would not be a problem. Basically then, to me at least, learning German was a pointless activity. I would never really need German in the real world. It was merely theoretical knowledge I had to acquire to pass a set of exams at the end of the year but which would have no bearing on my life beyond that. It was useless and irrelevant. Interesting at times, sure. But purely on an intellectual level. Really, I might as well have been learning Greenlandic Norse. I would never actually *need* it.

Because I felt that there was a disconnect between German class and real life, I was never really motivated to study it hard. In fact, most of the time I wished I didn't have to be there at all so that I could be using the time for something more worthwhile and meaningful.

I think the same thing can happen at church. There can be often be this feeling that all we're really doing on a Sunday morning is engaging in an abstract, intellectual pursuit and acquiring head knowledge which isn't really connected to anything that's going on around us. And that's largely because of the way that we're taught.

There are two basic ways we can teach the Bible.

## TOPICAL V EXPOSITORY

The first way of teaching the Bible is *topically*.

Topical teaching means picking a relevant subject and then drawing on verses from the entire Bible to build up an overall thesis on that subject. The topic may be "Angels and Demons", "Prayer", "Parenting", "Money", "Heaven". Anything really.

The second way of teaching the Bible is *expository*.

Expository teaching means systematically going through the individual books of the Bible verse-by-verse, chapter-by-chapter, book-by-book. The idea behind this method is that every part of the Bible will eventually be covered, the difficult or controversial passages won't be avoided, and most importantly, everything will be read and understood within its original grammatical, cultural and historical contexts.

Basically with topical teaching, you're starting with a relevant issue which you feel the church needs to hear about and then using the whole Bible to support the thesis. With expository, you're starting with the Word of God and pulling truths out of that to create the thesis.

Many churches and a particularly seminaries would argue that expository teaching is the *only* valid way to preach the Bible. They argue that topical preaching is too open to abuse and misinterpretation. They say that pastors could come up with a false thesis and then pluck verses from the Bible out of context to support it. They say that topical pastors can stick to populist messages and never tackle the more difficult, but equally necessary, parts of the Bible. They would argue that it is only through expository preaching that we really get to the author's real intended message. They would say that it's the only way to be sure we're not letting man set the agenda but that God's Word is taking precedence. This is an opinion that has gathered momentum and so there are many churches who never deviate from this way of teaching. It's expository *only* - strictly no topical preaching allowed.

Honestly, I think these people make good points. Expository preaching *does* help stop pastors from preaching their favourite topics all the time and leaving out the trickier parts (although I have been in churches where pastors have skipped or fudged chapters to avoid the tricky parts so this isn't a foolproof argument). Expository teaching *does* also help people understand context too. In fact, I'm very much *for* expository teaching. There is a lot to be said for it. However, I *am* against the idea of expository *only*. Because when we cling to expository *only*, I believe we can quickly create a disconnect between what's happening in church and what's happening in real life. It can start to feel like German class. Nothing but a scholastic exercise.

## The Disconnect

Let me explain.

Imagine a church is doing an expository study of the book of Isaiah. The people come to church the first week and they hear teaching from Isaiah 1. They then go out into the real world and something like the financial crisis may happen. Suddenly they have questions and concerns regarding the crumbling economy and what the Bible says about money. They take those questions with them to church the following Sunday and do they get answers there? No, they get Isaiah 2. Because that's the expository program the church is on and they're sticking to it. The following week, out in the real world there are tsunamis and earthquakes and reports of Christian persecution. Christians ask themselves valid questions like, "Why do Christians suffer? Are these the end times? What should we do if persecuted? How can we support our persecuted brothers and sisters in other areas? Is there anything practical we can do?" They take these questions to church the next Sunday and do they get answers? No, they get Isaiah 3. Because we're sticking to the program. The following week someone is told they have cancer and won't live much longer. Another is having parenting troubles with a tearaway teenager. They bring questions about these real problems to church but do they get answers? No, they get Isaiah 4. You get the picture.

The world is full of important topical issues right now. The Middle East situation begs questions about God's plan for Israel. The approval of gay marriage by our politicians raises questions about what real marriage is, why it's important and why God ordained it. Post-modernism begs questions about whether right and wrong are objective or subjective and whether all paths leads to heaven. It's not as though we don't have questions and challenges and problems. And it's not as though God doesn't have the answers. Indeed, God tells us to be watchful and to discern the signs of the times. But when we go to church there is often a disconnect between the real world with all its real problems and the teaching we receive. If the pastor isn't kicking at an open door by preaching the Gospel again, we're often just getting puffed up with head knowledge on Greek verb tenses or learning historical facts.

In some extreme cases expository pastors are known to spend whole sermons on a *single word* or up to an entire *decade* studying a *single book* of the Bible! How is this going to give anyone a comprehensive Biblical worldview from which to face the challenges of the day? For many then, an idea has emerged that church is merely an intellectual study which is interesting at times but largely irrelevant to what is actually happening in real life. We go into this building and leave the world behind for a couple of hours to get a lecture on a Sunday, and then we come out and get on with life again, having gained nothing that will really help us with Monday morning.

So we have to ask the question, "Is it really such a terrible thing to preach topically? Is it such a bad idea to give people answers to real problems? Is expository preaching really the only valid method?"

## Is Topical Preaching Wrong?

When we look through the Bible we find that Jesus himself preached...topically! When Jesus preached he didn't open up the scriptures at Exodus and then go through it verse-by-verse and chapter-by-chapter with his disciples. He preached about things that affected the people and used the scriptures to support what he was saying. The Sermon on the Mount was a topical sermon. First he teaches on the topic of Law, then Anger, then Adultery, then Divorce, then Vows, Revenge, Love For Enemies, Giving to the Needy, Money & Possessions,

Judgement and then Prayer. He dips into the scripture for reference points or support for what he's saying: "You have heard it said...." He preached like that all the way through his ministry. In fact, the last teaching he is recorded to have given was after his resurrection when he sat down with his disciples and took them through the scriptures, pointing out all the verses that revealed himself as the Messiah. (Luke 24:27) So from beginning to end, Jesus wanted to give people answers on important topics.

Even more than this, a lot of what Jesus talks about in the Gospels actually comes in response to direct questions from people in the crowd or from his disciples. "Teacher, I have this issue with paying taxes to Caesar. Should we do that?" "Teacher, what do you say about...." "Teacher, why does this happen?" "Teacher, is it right to...?" The people set the topic and then Jesus responds to these questions, sometimes with parables rather than verses, but often dipping into scripture to support his claims saying things like, "that is why the scriptures say..." or "Haven't you read the words of the prophets...?"

You'll notice this way of teaching is much less formal than what we're used to today. When was the last time you saw someone in a church congregation stand up and present the pastor with a question? I've never seen it! Safe to say that it doesn't happen at all generally. But if this is how Jesus preached and he allowed questions from the crowd, why don't we emulate him? Why don't we have interaction and participation? At least a bit of Q&A at the end? Jesus had real answers for real people on the real issues that concerned them and he allowed them to ask questions. Why is it that instead of following his example and doing what Jesus did, we now merely do a systematic, intellectual study about what Jesus did?

As you work through the rest of the New Testament you'll also discover that Paul's letters are topical. Read the epistles and you'll find they generally go along the lines of, "I hear you have this problem in your church. Well this is what God says about that..." Or, "I have heard reports of this kind of immorality in your church. This is my instruction on this matter..." Like Jesus, Paul directly addresses the issues which are facing the church of a particular town or region. He chastises. He exhorts. He reasons. And he uses scripture to support his position. Again, real ignorance is being corrected and real wrongs are being redressed.

People today have a genuine thirst for answers in a very confusing world. They're just looking in the wrong places for the answers because the church isn't giving them any. Is there any truth to the claims of evolution? Does the increase in wars and natural disasters mean we're in the last days? My grandparent just died, has she gone to heaven? My pet just died, has it gone to heaven? What will heaven actually be like? Should we vote? How should I handle money? Is hell real? Where was God when that tsunami hit last week? These are real questions from real people, for which the Bible has real answers, but the church often doesn't supply them. The come-and-watch format of our Sunday services means you get the show and the message that has been prepared for that week and nothing more. It is designed for you to stay passive. Simply to watch and listen, feel emotional at the right moments and dutifully volunteer for some of our pre-approved programs. This should not be so.

I have noticed that topical sermon series are the most appealing for the church and the ones that people get most excited about. They are the most well-attended. And that's simply because they seem the most relevant to real life. They bring direction, hope, encouragement and answers to a church which is currently facing bewildering problems, marginalisation and persecution. Christians actually need this information.

## The Balance

Here's a blog by a man named Jonathan Leeman. It perhaps gives some balance to the whole issue.

*"Dear Mr. Young Expositional Preacher. I am a member of your church. Call me Johnny Average Church Member.*

*First of all, I am very grateful for your commitment to expositional preaching. Don't lose the commitment.*

*But I need your help. I'm trying really hard to be a better husband, and worker, and citizen, and parent, and to wear all the other hats I have to wear. I need to know how to be a man, how to fight stress, how to have a better prayer life, how to make a difference in my neighborhood. I mean, Greek verb tenses and Old Testament typological structures are sort of interesting to me, at least if it's one of those Sunday mornings when I'm pepped up on several cups of Joe.*

*Yet I'm trying to figure out what those things have to do with how I go to work on Monday, and how I speak to my little girl, and what I do with my money. These are the decisions that face me as soon as I walk out of your building. And I have to be honest with you, this is why those big mega-church guys and their topical sermons are appealing to me. They give it to me straight.*

*Now I know what you're thinking, because I've picked up some of your lingo on The Gospel Coalition website. You're thinking, "Johnny Average Church Member, it sounds like you're looking for 'how-to' moralism. I preach Christ-centered sermons!"*

*Yes, thank you, give me Christ-centered sermons. But if Jesus is Lord, shouldn't that fact affect how I go to work on Monday, and speak to my little girl, and spend my money? What does the gospel have to say to me in all those places? What does the gospel say to me about stress, and retirement, and serving in government, and talking to my friend with a gambling addiction?*

*It seems to me that your gospel-centered expositional sermons should get to all the stuff that topical preachers preach about, right? Your preaching should be giving people all that and more. I think you call it sermon "application." Shouldn't your applications make expositional sermons topical, so to speak? Shouldn't they, over time, cover all the topics of people's lives? Shouldn't the members in your church feel like they're not missing anything?*

*Okay, okay, I know there's still a huge difference between your average topical sermon and your average expositional sermon, which is crucial. The Bible doesn't exist, and church gatherings don't happen, and sermons aren't preached, simply to help people like me do this or that better. And a steady diet of topical preaching can make it seem that way—like the point of the whole church exercise is to improve my daily life. When really, the whole point of gathering and listening to preaching is to* behold God, and to hear whatever he wants to say. I know that. I know I need his Word exposed, no matter what it says. I know I need to hear all of it, even the parts that seem obscure and irrelevant.

I'm just saying that I need you to show me how those obscure bits are relevant, even if those Hebrew chiasms are as naturally fascinating to you as they are to my Sunday School teacher who doesn't get out much. I need you to show me how those chiasms help me to trust more, hope more, love more, and what that faith, hope, and love look like in the different areas of my life. Make sense?

Connect the dots for me. How do I get from justification by faith alone to being a manly man who cares well for his aging parents?

Okay, I admit, I don't really want you to give up the expositional thing. I just want more from you. I want to have my cake and to eat it, too. Call me biblically greedy. I want you to apply your sermon in my life so that I'm learning all the helpful stuff they're learning over at Topical Tommy's church. Okay?

Thanks for listening, Mr. Young Expositional Preacher. For real, I thank God for you, and the fact that you've chosen the harder, more faithful path."

(http://www.9marks.org/blog/maybe-i-do-want-topical-preaching)

There are merits to expositional preaching which we must not lose sight of but we must also never lose sight of the fact that people need real answers. To that end, we must emulate Jesus and Paul in the way that they taught.

I think it's worth referring to Mark Driscoll here, the pastor of Mars Hill Church in Seattle. Driscoll allows people to text questions during the sermon. At the end of his message a few of the questions come up on the screen and without having any forewarning, he ends up delving into issues that others normally wouldn't normally broach, such as sex and pornography for example. The fact that he dares to take these questions on and talks about such things from the platform has created much controversy. Many people have criticised him for talking about such unseemly things in church. Like real issues and authenticity with one another is not for the church setting. Like we must just keep up the superficial, pretentious, churchy facade, pretend everything's alright and keep hiding our problems and our sin from one another. If we can't be real with fellow-Christians then when can we be? Driscoll is just meeting people's real questions with real answers. And of course, they are responding to it as Mars Hill continues to be one of the fastest growing churches in the United States. The people go there knowing they're going to get some connection with the issues that are actually affecting them.

*Relevance* is not a bad word. God has answers. The Bible has answers. The world just doesn't know about them. The church needs to be empowered with this knowledge so that we can be bold and courageous in telling the world about it.

# Chapter 11

# The Story So Far

---

We've nearly finished our deconstruction of the church but before we move onto the last chapter, let's stop to do a quick review of the kind of church that is starting to emerge.

In the first chapter we learned that we need to be constantly challenged to grow and progress so we need deep teaching. In order to make sure everyone gets access to teaching that matches their level of understanding and that no one gets left behind, it may make sense to break down the overall church into smaller discipleship groups - in the same way we break whole schools down into classes of no more than 30 per teacher. This means everyone can be given personal attention and mentored in the right way. We then saw how these small groups should learn by doing - this is true discipleship. No passive bystanders allowed. We saw how the leader of these small discipleship groups should literally lead by example like Jesus did. Leaders shouldn't ask their disciples to do anything they're not prepared to do first. They should provide the example for the others to follow. The aim of this is to mature and empower the disciples to a level where they can then lead groups of their own. So that they can lead groups of their own. So that they can lead groups of their own. This self-replicating system leads to explosive, persecution-proof growth. We learned these small groups should operate in a kind of tidal motion. Come in, go out, come in, go out. As they go out to apply what they're learning, the problems of self-righteous pride, pointless bickering, hard-heartedness and hypocrisy in worship are overcome. Instead the church learns true humility, deep unity, an increase of faith, productivity for the Kingdom of God and benefits from other forms of sanctification. Furthermore, and very importantly, the world will then be reached by a practical, adventurous, loving and courageous faith which wins souls, brings hope and love to battered, cynical people, and halts social decline and immorality.

We learned that teaching times should be relevant and responsive to the real issues that people are facing. Furthermore, people should be free to ask questions and receive answers in church. If that leads to confrontation and debate then so be it. As long as the end goal is to discover the truth and then to apply it in practical ways. We also learned that we should dispense with idolatrous, stale traditions and our Churchianity. There's no reason to go through the same rituals for the sake of it and to the contrary, we need to start acting authentically, spontaneously, extravagantly and with honesty. We need radical ideals and uncompromising attitudes. We also learned that if the church is to be a city on a hill shining for all the world to see, it must clean up its act and pursue righteousness first. This is because the Holy Spirit needs to be driving our efforts and if He isn't there, we may find ourselves falling into the fleshly or demonic instead. The church needs to set goals and to work together to achieve them.

Words that may describe this model church are "informal", "community", "practical", "loving", "confrontational", "authentic", "extravagant", "risk-taking", "self-replicating", "unified", "challenged", "courageous", "relevant", "righteous" and "responsive".

With that general image of church in your mind, let's finish up this section with one more point.

# Chapter 12

# We Have Lost Our Men

---

If there is any demographic within church that is more restless than the rest, it's men. In fact, so restless are the men that they aren't even there! Statistics show that there are more women than men in every type of church in every part of the world. Roughly, for every 6 or 7 women, you will only find 3 or 4 men. Most young men will leave the church before they turn 20 and although some will return in their 30s with a wife and kids in tow, many won't return at all. This means that in many churches, single women now outnumber guys by around 2 to 1. You only need to look around to see the evidence.

Why is the church haemorrhaging men?

David Murrow has spent a lot of time examining this issue and says, "There are only two possible explanations for the lack of men in church – either A) men are more sinful than women, or B) there's something about the church that's driving men away. The more I study men and church, the more I'm convinced "B" is the more likely cause."

In short, he agrees with what many other commentators have been saying for a long time - the church has been "feminized". The church is now an environment that many men don't fit into and don't want to be a part of.

To prove the point, Murrow conducted an exercise where he showed two lists to hundreds of people, Christian and non-

Christian. He asked them to identify the list that they thought best characterised Jesus and his true followers:

| LEFT SET | RIGHT SET |
|---|---|
| Competence | Love |
| Power | Communication |
| Efficiency | Beauty |
| Achievement | Relationships |
| Skills | Support |
| Proving oneself | Help |
| Results | Nurturing |
| Accomplishment | Feelings |
| Objects | Sharing |
| Technology | Relating |
| Goal-oriented | Harmony |
| Self-sufficiency | Community |
| Success | Loving cooperation |
| Competition | Personal expression |

More than 95% of the time, Murrow says people chose the Right Set as the best representation of true Christian values. The shocker is that Murrow created the two lists using words taken from John Gray's book, *"Men Are From Mars, Women Are From Venus"*. The left set are the traditional values of men and the right set are the traditional values of women. Murrow's point is that when people think of Christ and His followers, they automatically think of feminine values.

When men pick up on this, even subconsciously, the reaction to attending church is similar to the reaction they might have if asked to attend a bridal shower or a bachelorette party. They want nothing to do with it. In general, men are looking for an environment where they can express their masculinity. That's why they go to the outdoors, to physical sporting events and to hardware stores. Men want to be men but they don't feel like they can be at church. They feel like there's no place for them there.

Why is this at all important? Why do we need men in church?

Well, it's not just that masses of Christian girls are growing up without suitable partners, as problematic as that is. The church is suffering in many other ways from the absence of men. To understand how, we need to explore exactly what masculinity is. Only then, will we understand what we're missing.

Defining masculinity, or femininity for that matter, is a risky business. As soon as I start to do this I will inevitably cause offence to someone, somewhere who believes their masculinity or femininity is being undermined by generalised stereotypes to which they don't fully conform. In other words you may find yourself starting sentences in the next few minutes with "but I'm a woman and I don't..." or "but I'm a man and I've never...." "Does that make me less of a man/woman?" Nevertheless, it would be foolish to perpetuate the secular idea that there is no basic difference between the sexes. It's important to realise that men and women are indeed very different, were designed by God to be different, that the differences are good and that they complement one another. While each man or woman won't fit all the generalisations exactly, and while that doesn't make them any less of a man or woman, there are indeed inherent traits and natural tendencies within the sexes that we would be foolish to ignore.

## Rules & Relationships

When I was a kid I used to play tennis with my sister but with a twist that always used to frustrate me - she would never play competitively. Ever. She just wasn't interested in keeping score; she only wanted to "play rallies". I didn't get it. What was the point in knocking the ball back and forth over the net for hours if there was no winning and losing? I couldn't see the appeal in this. She only ever wanted to play a kind of co-operative game where we worked together to see how long we could keep the ball going back and forth without it going out of play. Me, on the other hand, I *wanted* the ball to go out of play! Preferably after an overhead smash or a drilled forehand down the line. That's what gave me a thrill.

I preferred playing tennis with my best friend, Brendan. He was a guy and with guys it was at least competitive. In fact, at times it got so competitive that we would get into some pretty big arguments. If I hit a winner close to the line and Brendan called it 'out' (as he had a habit of doing) the game would instantly have to come to a stop until we debated the decision. Sometimes for ten to fifteen minutes or more. In fact, I'm pretty sure that one time I felt so cheated I walked off the court and refused to play on. You'll see this dynamic in pretty much any playground or field where boys are playing together. The games boys play are generally competitive and before any action takes place they will come together to meticulously lay the rules down and map out the boundaries. Rules are *very* important to boys. They simply cannot be violated. If one boy feels like the rules of the game have been violated the whole thing will have to come to a stop until the call has been argued out. Obeying the rules is so important to boys that if one feels a strong sense of injustice, he may even pick up the ball, leave his friends, and go home. In other words, boys will sacrifice relationships on the altar of rules. Rules are the *most* important thing.

Girls playing together are far less interested in rules and are far more interested in co-operation and relationships. Like my sister who, even though we were on opposite sides of the tennis net, wanted to play a co-operative game so that there were no winners or losers. Girls like to jump rope where two hold either end and another goes in the middle to see how long they can skip for without getting tangled up. They'll play relational fantasy games where one pretends to be the mummy and another pretends to be the daddy. Often they'll just sit and chat about something. There are rarely winners and losers in girls games. They're simply about building relationships. In fact, when they find themselves amongst competitive boys who are arguing about rules, you'll often hear them protesting, "what does it matter, it's only a game!" They just want everyone to get along and play nicely. This is a mindset that boys generally can't comprehend. Therefore, contrary to boys, girls will sacrifice rules on the altar of relationships. Relationships are the *most* important thing.

As boys and girls grow up into men and women the basic traits remain. When a man is grappling with a dilemma his first question is, "what do the rules say?" When a woman is grappling with a dilemma, the first question they ask is, "how will this decision affect my relationships?" Men continue to be more concerned with right and wrong while girls continue to be more concerned with unity.

For example, even in adulthood, men will continue to argue about sporting decisions. Sometimes the arguments last for years or even decades after they were made. Fair play and justice is paramount. "Was his foot over the line?" "Did the referee get the call right?" "Where did the ball land?" English and German football fans to this day will debate whether the ball was over the line in the 1966 World Cup Final. Men actually don't care if someone wins or loses by a decision as long as everything was done according to the rules, fair play was observed and justice was served.

Women on the other hand continue to be obsessed with relationships into adulthood. Their favourite books, movies and magazines usually revolve around relationships of one kind or another. Women also continue to be more likely to plan social events and to keep up with extended family and old friends.

While we're on this subject, here's a little sidetrack. You may remember in *Know Your Enemy* I pointed out that Truth had to come before Unity. Well because men are naturally more concerned with Truth (i.e. the rules), and women more concerned with Unity (i.e. relationships), this is one of the reasons that God designated men to lead. Because Truth must come before Unity. When women lead and Unity becomes more important than right and wrong, quite often there is a slide into liberalism and heresy. An example of Unity before Truth is, *"God is love. These two men love each other. Why should we not bless their relationship? Jesus never excluded anyone and stood with the downtrodden and oppressed."* In other words, "what does right and wrong matter as long as these people want to be together? Isn't Unity, peace and love the most important thing?" Jesus did indeed stand with the downtrodden and oppressed but always within the boundaries set by the moral law. Jesus was absolutely unwavering in his demands for purity and righteousness. Truth must come first and then we need to Unite behind that truth. The natural tendency for men to put Truth ahead of Unity means they must lead. Now you could argue, "if excessive female led focus on unity leads to liberalism, then doesn't excessive male led focus on rules lead to legalism?" That would be correct. Which is why, to avoid both pits, we need both men and women working together. And both are equally important. But Truth must come before Unity. And so the masculine must lead out. If that means picking up the ball and walking away from sections of church that are approving gay marriage and blaspheming the name of God, then so be it.

## RISK TAKERS & COMFORT CREATORS

Men are more likely to thrive when they feel challenged while women are more likely to thrive when they feel secure. Men are warriors and adventurers. They want battles to fight. They want goals to strive for. They want to expend their lives for a greater cause. It's hardwired into them. They don't want safety and security. They don't want domesticity. They want to leave behind the comfortable and the suburban and find themselves in the wilds. Look at the stories men love. They normally always involve these three elements:

1. An *adventure*/quest/greater purpose for which they're willing to lay down their lives.
2. A *battle* to fight along the way.
3. A *beauty* to fight for.

Think of Star Wars. An *adventure* across the galaxy, *battling* against the evil empire and rescuing *beautiful* Princess Leia. Or Braveheart - an *adventure* across Scotland, *battling* the evil King Edward, avenging the death of *beautiful* Murron. Gladiator - an *adventure* across the Roman Empire, *battling* the cruel Emperor Commodus, avenging the death of his *beautiful* wife. The James Bond franchise - *adventures* across the world, *battling* an arch-villain, rescuing the *beautiful* girl. The stories don't always contain all the elements but they contain at least one or two of the three. These are the things men crave.

They want to be challenged. They want to be moved out of their comfort zone. They want mountains to conquer. They want problems to solve physically or mentally. They want to take risks and for their strength to be tested. They want something bracing or demanding. They want to be the hero. Why does a man want to go through all the hardship involved in trekking to the North Pole or climbing Everest or swimming the Channel or running a marathon or exploring a jungle? Simply because he can and because that's what he is. It's what he was designed by God to be.

Men were also made by God to be creators. Men want to build things. Engines, bridges, rafts, computer programs, businesses, sheds, furniture, families. They want to attempt risky projects. Then once the thing has been created, there's an endless desire to improve it or cultivate it. They want to add extensions to their buildings, add more horsepower to their engines, add more features to their computer programs etc. Guys love a hardware store because it appeals to this desire to create, build, manufacture and improve. The job is never done.

Men also desperately want authenticity. They don't mind if you if you argue with them or confront them as long as you're being real with them. They want to hear the truth and they're not too concerned about how you tell them, as long as they can see it's for the greater cause. On the football field you'll often hear guys tearing strips off each other verbally but then once the game comes to an end they'll shake hands and it's all forgotten. Guys talk in a more direct manner than girls.

Now all of these things - the search for competition, adventure, risk, initiation, authenticity and demanding challenges naturally forces the man to look ever outward. It causes him to search for new territories, new horizons, new adventures, new battles, new kingdoms, new opponents, new projects, uncharted waters. That outward focus is incredibly important.

*And that's what we've lost in the church.*

The feminized church isn't so interested in any of that. Women prefer to be secure and safe. It's under those conditions that women generally thrive. So the feminized church starts to look inward and becomes more concerned with relational activities, unity, peace-making, ecumenism, therapy, feelings, harmony, nurturing and emotional care. It looks to create comfort and security instead. Nancy Pearcey wrote, "*...many people think of church only as a nurturing place that addresses personal needs. Think: sitting in circles, sharing feelings, holding hands, singing softly, comforting members. An example of the feminization of the church is its music. Typical praise songs refer to Jesus as a Christian's lover and praise his beauty and tenderness. Rarely do they praise his justice or strength, or refer to him as the head of an army leading his church into spiritual battle, like "Onward Christian Soldiers."*

(Here's Tim Hawkins also making this point - http://www.youtube.com/watch?v=mva4_xhFLVI)

The inward facing, feminine Christian disciplines are not bad in themselves - in fact, they are vital - in the tidal motion of discipleship the coming in to be nourished and cared for is just as important as the going out, but when the outward facing masculine disciplines disappear altogether, there is less room for evangelism, hard debate, practical application, moral judgements, achievement, goal-oriented endeavours and other such things. Things that men thrive on. Men look at what's left in the church - the holding hands, sharing feelings in circles, singing songs about touching Jesus' face - and it doesn't appeal to them and they can't see where they're needed. Indeed, they often find their masculinity stigmatised in the church, as it is in the wider culture. Hence, the church is losing its creators, risk takers, warriors, leaders and adventurers. The church needs authentic community and good relationships - things women are great at - but it needs those things *as it goes out* to change the world. Otherwise it becomes too insular and all the problems we've been discussing in this book start to materialise.

Bojidar Marinov writes, *"Why would a young man stay in the church? Is there a "male" message in our churches today? Is there a message that gives a young man a worthy cause to work for and to fight for? Why would he stay, to listen all his life to the same sermon over and over again, in many different versions of it? Come back every Sunday to learn - for the nth time, over and over again - that God loves us? Shed tears over the same emotional stuff every week?...There is no message for [men]. The church's message concerns only the church and the limited scope of activities that the pastors have declared to be "spiritual"...Why would he want to stay in a church, passive, listening to the same sermon every Sunday that tells him there is nothing he can do to change the world?...He is eager to go out there and prove himself in many fields but then the church is silent about them...There is no theology for political action, no theology for business action, no theology for social activity...The silence and refusal of the churches to preach and teach a comprehensive worldview creates a tension; and our young men resolve the tension by leaving the church and going to the world...it is a perfectly logical response to the deficiencies in our church's preaching and teaching...This hasn't always been the case. Two or three centuries ago...the American church had a message of victory, a message that it was a city on a hill, and by its example God would change the world for Christ. Men like Cotton Mather preached on political and economic issues (Fair Dealings Between Debtor and Creditor is one example); and the civil government was constantly under scrutiny and criticism from the pulpits. The churches did not wait for their boys to go out and find worthy causes. The churches led the boys in those worthy causes in their crusade to redeem the world for Christ. . . And young men stayed in the churches, and built Christian families, and expanded the Kingdom of God, and built the Christian culture that we today thank God for. . . That should tell us how we can take our young men back. As long as we have a female church with a female message, our young men will prefer to stay away from it."*

The men who would drive the church out of its comfort zone and lead it into dangerous territories; The ones who would take the church into spiritual battle; The ones who would take risks and attempt scary things for the Kingdom of God; The ones who would have the courage to build and cultivate Godly families, are largely no longer there.

## Feelers & Doers

Nancy Pearcey again says, *"Another turn-off for men is touchy-feely sermons. The modern church stresses emotions and inner spiritual experiences while neglecting the intellectual side of the faith.*

*The more traditionally masculine side of Christianity enjoys crossing swords with hostile secular worldviews. So, as long as*

*Christianity appeals to the emotional, therapeutic, interpersonal, relational areas, it's not going to appeal to men as much as to women.*

*Churches should engage men's intellects to help them see the relevance of Christianity to the "real" world of politics, industry and business.*

*We have to recover the notion that Christianity is true on all levels, not just for your emotional life or repairing relationships, as important as those things are,"*

In other words, guys don't just want to know how Christianity makes them feel; they want to know how it applies to the real world. Men love apologetics, theology, philosophy, ethics, science and history. They want to see a connection between all those things and the real world and they want to know what they can do to change things. In the first chapter we talked about how feelings are not the end goal of Christianity. And if Christianity is defined simply as an emotional experience on a Sunday morning, it's going to appeal more to girls than boys.

Nancy Pearcey confirms what we've been learning saying, ""*Men are more attracted to religion if it presented as a quest, an adventure, a heroic exploit. They want something challenging, bracing, demanding."*

Men want someone to throw the gauntlet down to them. They go to church and they don't get it. They're asked to sit and passively watch the show. To hear things they already know. And then are berated for not feeling emotional enough about it.

David Murrow says, "Men want to expend their lives for a great cause, even if it involves risk."

Now here's the important point. The great cause exists! In fact the great cause is the whole reason the church exists! It's talked about in the Bible; it's commanded by Jesus; it's even given the title "the Great Commission". It is the greatest cause there is. But there is little impetus towards it in the church. Nothing is demanded of the man in church. He is never given something to fight for. He's not made aware of the real spiritual battle between good and evil. As he looks around a fuschia and lemon yellow sanctuary with nice floral displays and sees people being implored, by way of a milky sermon, to just feel more emotional, sing songs about touching Jesus' face, then left to go home, he wonders if he has anything to offer and he is often bored and restless in the meantime.

The men who built the New Testament church were ordinary guys. Fishermen mainly. But because they had been given something to go after and were empowered by the Spirit they confronted evil, endured beatings, led from the front, overturned kingdoms, enforced justice, stopped the mouths of lions and ultimately changed the world. These are the kind of men the church needs. The creators, the risk takers, the warriors, the defenders, the entrepreneurs, the innovators, the initiative takers, the adventurers. These are the guys that have left because they have formed an impression that church is for women and children only.

Mark Driscoll once controversially said that many of the guys who are left in church are not the creators and cultivators that it needs, but are instead cowards and complainers. These are the guys who are content to passively watch a show every week because they are too afraid to do anything else. Driscoll says that as these guys look on, they tend to turn into complainers. He says, *"the notorious sin of Christian guys is complaining about guys who are doing things rather than doing something themselves."* It's a lot harder to do something than it is to complain about those who are doing something. In Christian circles you'll find that when one guy goes out to win hundreds or thousands of souls for Christ, there are generally a bunch of other guys complaining about how he did it. I've experienced this since starting the Fuel Project. *"Why didn't you use my version of the Bible?" "The music you used on that sounded kinda worldly to me." "You used a quotation by a guy I don't like."* Complaining is so much easier than doing something. The rule of thumb should always be, if you think you've got a better way, then go make it happen.

## ANOTHER BLOG

Let me finish off this chapter by referring to a blog from a man who has decided to stop going to Sunday services. He highlights many of the themes we've been talking about here.

*"Men aren't attending church! This is the cry of panic among many organized church attendees. There has been a rapid decline in the number of men attending church services. This decline has caused many leaders within religious institutions to embark on a search for answers. They are desperate to find some kind of method they can apply or program they can start that will draw men back into their institutions. This endeavor to get men back into religious gatherings has been the subject matter of countless articles in popular Christian magazines, the theme of some recently released books, and the hot topic on numerous Christian on-line forums. Well, I wanted to take some time to share my thoughts on the matter. I'm a man who doesn't attend church services, so I guess I can present the other point of view to some degree.*

*Let me lay it out flat. There is no new style of preaching, no sermon, no program you can introduce, no musical styling you can bring into worship that would bring me back. There's no secret formula you have to crack to understand my mind so you can appeal to me. No gimmick, no game, no special event you need. I'm not somebody's trophy to be won through clever outreach tools. I'm not a potential pew filler, chair warmer, sermon listener, or ministry need filler. Religious meetings and services have no appeal to me at all whatsoever.*

*So what does appeal to me? Jesus. Plain and simple. Jesus. No agenda, no sermons, no services, no ministries, no organizations, just this amazing guy named Jesus. And I like people who are real. And I especially like people who are real and are really in love with Jesus.*

*But see, I don't think Jesus is in such a rush to get men into services as many folks are. He hung with men by the sea shore. He fished with them. He ate with them. He even hung out with the scum bags and laughed with them. He never told them to get somewhere or be somewhere. He went to them in the real world. And He didn't come with the motive of being with them until He could get them to join something or be a part of something. He knew how to be a friend. He was real. He wasn't offended by them. He didn't judge them. He just accepted them. And then when He turned and said "follow me" He didn't lead them into a church service. He lead them to walk on water, cast out demons, go to prison for Him, be broken, beaten black and blue and to be killed. But He never sat them down in a church service.*

*No, services have no appeal to me. I don't need soft carpet under my feet or nice sermons in my ears. What I crave, want, and yearn for is the real life of Christ lived out in the real world in raw reality. You can't manufacture this in a meeting or develop a strategy for this. Either you've got Jesus or you don't. Either His life is real in you or it's not. I don't care what works within the four walls of a Sunday morning meeting. If I doesn't work out here in the real world, then it doesn't mean a hill of beans to me.*

*I have found that many Christians are held captive within a mindset that church is either "my way or the highway." I don't believe Jesus nor scriptures ever taught that church is a once a week meeting, a religious organization, or a building with a cross on top. What is the church? It is the people who follow Jesus. Now we know this theologically, but like many things we know theologically the reality of that is just not there for many folks. See, not attending a once a week religious meeting does not mean I have "left church." If church is the people who follow Jesus, and I am a person who follows Jesus, the only way I can leave church is by leaving Him. Being His church is based on His choosing me, not on my attendance to a meeting.*

*So does not belonging to a religious organization mean that I'm a "Lone Ranger?" The truth is, anybody with a growing and thriving relationship with Jesus is drawn to be around people more and to connect with people in deeper ways. I have established, and am establishing many relationships with other believers that are very Christ centered and very real. Jesus said where two or more are gathered there He is. So anytime I'm with these folks, Jesus is there and we are simply being His church. We pray together, talk about what He's doing in our lives, encourage one another, correct each other, and spur each other on in our walk with Him. But it's not programmed. It happens naturally in our daily lives so there is such a raw reality to it. We are living things that all my years in Sunday morning meetings tried to accomplish, but all the organization and programs seemed to get in the way of the reality of it.*

*So by leaving church services am I saying I don't want to be around the body of Christ? Heavens no! Just the opposite. I have such a desire to be connected with the body of Christ that I got tired of the structures and meetings getting in the way of building authentic relationships. See, the question I ask is through all of the Sunday morning services and meetings, are Christians really connecting with the body? Sure they are in midst of the body, but are they connecting? If you took away the Sunday service and got rid of the building, would the relationships continue? Or were they built around an organization or a structure? Can people connect without a man up front telling them when and how to connect? Or do they look to the religious machinery to orchestrate and organize life as God's family?*

*So am I hurt or offended? No way! The belief that if somebody doesn't attend or belong to a religious organization means they are bitter, hateful or angry is an old stereotype that really needs to be put to death. Sometimes I think that stereotype is used as a form of manipulation and control to keep people attending religious meetings, that in honesty, many folks are bored to tears with. (Not everybody.) Who wants to be viewed as bitter, hateful or offended? Jesus called us to a life of knowing and enjoying Him. But sadly, for many (especially men) religious duties and obligations suck the joy right out of following Jesus.*

*Do we serve God by what we do? Or by knowing Him? That is the real question. I hear Martha calling from the kitchen of religious obligation, "Lord make them get in here and help us." But Jesus said Mary chose the better part that would not be taken away from her.*

*This isn't about "us verses them." If attending a Sunday morning meeting works for you, then fine! Go for it! But there are many folks that it doesn't. For them it's just dead works. So if they don't want to do that, then fine too! Remember, that meeting is not the church. The people are, whether they attend a weekly meekly meeting or not. And meetings should never be the measuring stick that we use to assess somebody's heart for God or concern for His people.*

*Of course at some point the question is always asked of us non-attenders, "What about ministry? How will you use your gifts if you don't go to church?" Well, does somebody have to attend a weekly Sunday morning meeting in order to minister to other Christians or receive from others? Is that meeting the church? See, I believe the people are the church, not a meeting. So the key is learning to live as the church through our daily lives. Absolutely, we should be encouraging and ministering to one another. But is a formal weekly meeting the only way that happens? (The truth is only a handful of people even have the opportunity to minister in those meetings.) Can this not happen through real relationships with one another? What about having other believers over for dinner? Is that not the church gathering together? What about sitting down with some brothers or sisters in Christ over lunch? Didn't Jesus say He'd be in the middle of that? What we Christians have done is drawn up little compartments for God. We say that this one meeting once a week is spiritual time and when true ministry happens, then we view everything else as inferior to that time. But I don't believe that at all. In fact, through looking at the life of Jesus and His relationships with those around Him, I personally believe what happens living relationally throughout the week with other believers is far more impacting than a weekly service. It was as Jesus and His followers were going from place to place among the people that He shaped their lives. I believe lives are shaped through genuine relationships, not weekly services. And the deepest ministry happens through relationship, not services.*

*If men are following Jesus, they aren't leaving church because church is what they are, not a place they go or a meeting they attend. If men stay out of religious organizations, yeah, the organizations may eventually die. But if the church (the people) aren't finding life in these things, maybe they need to shrivel up and die. Jesus said that He would build His church. Perhaps what we have been building and what He is building are two very different things. Just some thoughts from a man who doesn't attend "church" because he decided to be the church instead."*

*http://familyroommedia.com/Articles8.html*

According to George Barna, between 1994 and 2004, men's attendance at organised church services flat-lined. But during that same period, their participation in small groups doubled! It seems like many men are leaving the institutional church to seek out Jesus. This blogger appears to be representing an increasing minority.

## HAVE YOU NOTICED?

Now have you noticed that what guys crave is exactly what the church needs?

I have to admit that when I first started writing this book I didn't know what I was going to write for this chapter. I knew what I wanted to say for each of the preceding chapters but for this one I had nothing. In fact, I toyed with leaving this chapter out altogether because I didn't know where to begin or how to condense such a large issue into such a small space. But there was something that told me this was important and couldn't be ignored. I feel like I've only done a very rough and incomplete overview of the topic - the whole concept of masculinity and femininity in church is a book unto itself - but as I've researched the whole issue and started writing it, I began to see something I didn't expect to see. Everything that men want to be, and everything that men naturally are, is exactly what the church is missing.

Doug Giles wrote in what seems to be a typically brash style, *"Our times demand strong men and the church should be producing them, not repelling them. The Church needs men, who start a ministry or start a business; who get involved in politics, the arts and education; who are not afraid of the secular thugs and pimps who try to keep Christians marginalized in a religious ghetto."*

Speaking to Christian men directly he exhorts them not to back away saying, *"Go find your Holy Grail; go meet the strange, meet the unfamiliar. Protect people; lead people; rescue people; fight inequities and absurdities. Beware, young man, of parents and pastors who want to "mother" you. You need to avoid the secure, you need to fear over-protection and accept happily the masculine task of being the patriarch, prophet, warrior and wild man. Get to a place, young warrior, where pain is not a big deal, where you embrace resistance. Then, by your example you will encourage others to resist self-doubt, squeamishness, indecision and the impulse to surrender and withdraw into the warm, wet womb of Wussville."*

## The Women Will Still Be There

Forgive me for the lack of balance in this chapter. I haven't extolled the virtues of femininity nearly enough and I have placed far more emphasis on the men. But please note that I am not trying to turn church into a kind of boys club. This isn't about taking the feminine out of the church at all; it's just about re-dressing the balance by putting the masculine back in. The church needs its men back.

And to be honest, it seems to me that the kind of men the church needs are exactly the kind of men women want. If men start to live out their strength, take responsibility, learn to lead, act on convictions, take risks and become innovators, the women will be there because these are dateable and marriage-worthy guys. These are the kind of guys that women in church currently lament the lack of.

Ross Sawyers said, *"I have read that if a child comes to Christ, 12% of the time the family will follow. If the mom comes, there's a 15% chance the family will. But if the man comes to Christ, 90% of the time the family will come along behind."*

*Further Reading: Wild At Heart by John Eldredge*

# Section 2
# Reconstruction

# CHAPTER 13

# What Did The Early Church Actually Look Like?

In an excavation, archaeologists pull away dirt and rubble to reveal something original and glorious underneath. That's a picture of what I've been attempting in the first section of this book. We've been pulling away all the debris and man-made pollution that has accumulated around the church for hundreds of years in an attempt to bring into view original Christianity as it was known to the New Testament believers. We've been trying to dismantle the often unexamined rituals and traditions so that only the Biblical church that Jesus intended is left.

If I've done my job correctly you should now have quite a good image in your mind of what that Biblical church is supposed to look like. A new picture should already be coming into view. You should have an idea of something more authentic, dynamic, extravagant, spontaneous, powerful, righteous, practical, loving and true. Something which much more closely matches the church we read about when we open up the pages of the Bible.

## The Jehovah's Witnesses

But therein lies a question. What church *do* we read about when we open up the pages of the Bible?

Francis Chan tells a story of when a couple of Jehovah's Witnesses came knocking on his door. They got into a theological discussion which eventually came down to one basic idea. He told them, *"you guys believe that Michael, the Archangel, is the same person as Jesus Christ himself. But there's no way on earth you can look me in the eyes right now and tell me that you actually came before God one day and said, 'God show me the truth', and then you read the Bible for yourself, and then at the end of it you came to the conclusion that Jesus and Michael the Archangel are the same person. There's no way you can tell me that! Someone fed that to you because you would never get that just from reading the Bible. And so I just encouraged them saying 'look, I don't want to tell you what to believe, I'm not going to feed you something else. I'm just encouraging you to get alone with the Word of God, pray to God, and say "God, show me the truth", and then read it. See what conclusions you would come to.' It was a really good discussion. But after they left I started thinking to myself, 'was I really fair to them?' I mean, did I really do that myself? Did I really one day say, 'I really want to know the truth' and then sit down with the Word of God and begin to study and come to these conclusions? Honestly, that's now how it happened for me and a lot of things were fed to me as well. And so I've been on this journey thinking, 'if I were on an island and I just read [the Bible] over and over again, and it was the only influence I had, what would I believe just from my readings and studies of this book? Would I come up with church the way we do it in America? Probably not."*

Most of us are in the same position. We've grown up believing things that we didn't get from the Bible itself. I want to encourage you to do the same experiment where you forget about traditions and cultural norms, forget about what your parents or grandparents did, forget about what is comfortable for you or what you would prefer to be true and just sit down with the Bible and think, "what does this Book actually say?

What kind of church does this Book actually portray?" And then change based on what you read.

That's what I'm going to do in this chapter and I invite you to come with me on the journey. I'm going to simply open up the Book of Acts - the book that describes the activities of the early church after Jesus' ascension, and using the Bible alone, I'm going walk through it noting down the features and activities described within. As I keep noting down features, an overall picture should emerge. A fresh image of church should come into view.

Remember, all we need is a radical group of believers who are simply willing to look at the Bible and say, "forget the traditions, forget the clichéd images, the current paradigm, the way things have always been, forget who wins or loses by this...what does the Bible *actually* say? Let's do that."

## They Formed A Community

*"They all met together and were constantly united in prayer..."* - Acts 1:14

*"All the believers devoted themselves to the apostles' teaching, and to fellowship, and to sharing in meals (including the Lord's Supper), and to prayer.*

*A deep sense of awe came over them all, and the apostles performed many miraculous signs and wonders. And all the believers met together in one place and shared everything they had. They sold their property and possessions and shared the money with those in need. They worshiped together at the Temple each day, met in homes for the Lord's Supper, and shared their meals with great joy and generosity—all the while praising God and enjoying the goodwill of all the people. And each day the Lord added to their fellowship those who were being saved." - Acts 2:42-47*

There's a few ideas to draw out from these passages but the main one that really comes through is that the believers formed a community. In fact, in some translations of the Bible you'll see a subtitle in Acts 2 which says, *"The Believers Form A Community"* or something similar. The dictionary describes a community as *"a social, religious, occupational, or other group sharing common characteristics or interests and perceived or perceiving itself as distinct in some respect from the larger society within which it exists."*

So these Christians were a group of people who were still visible within society, but who were made distinct by unique characteristics and common interests. They were *in* the world but they were distinct from it. They were easily recognised by their shared characteristics. What were these characteristics?

Well, these verses tell us that the people within the community met constantly. In fact the Bible tells us that gatherings were happening every single day. You see, when people love one another, they naturally want to be together. Since the church was rightly characterised by love (John 13:35), they used to spend a lot of time in each other's company. They created an informal, extended family type of atmosphere. Christians today are generally happy to spend an hour in each other's company on a Sunday morning at a formal service and no more. Even that can sometimes be a push. And we don't particularly want to shake the hand of the stranger next to us or say hello to them while we're there. This betrays our lukewarm feelings towards one another and our lack of real community. The culture around us has become very individualistic and the church has followed suit. This should not be so. While our modern lifestyles may preclude us from *daily* gatherings, there should be more of a sense of genuine fellowship among the church and that should make us distinct. We should be known and recognised by our love for each other.

The Bible tells us what went on at these gatherings. There was prayer, worship, teaching, fellowship and food. You may be surprised at how often food is mentioned in relation to the meetings. Indeed, their gatherings often centred around an evening meal in someone's home. People would each prepare something to bring along. There would be meats, vegetables, fruits, cheese, wine etc. And they would all share in what was brought, enjoying one another's company in the process. In the midst of this eating there would be a moment of remembrance where bread would be broken and wine would be drunk to commemorate the Lord's death and resurrection. When we think of the Lord's supper today we think of a tiny square of stale bread and a thimble of juice or wine as part of a silent, structured Sunday morning service. The Lord's supper, as practiced in the early church however, was an actual supper! Again, it was much more informal and authentic and communal. Indeed in 1 Corinthians 11, it describes so much food and drink being present that some were overindulging and getting drunk. This behaviour was rightly condemned by Paul but it gives insight into the informality of these gatherings. They were like big cosy family meals.

Around this meal there would be a time of teaching, discussion, worship and prayer. In this way they experienced complete nourishment of soul and spirit as well as body. 1 Corinthians 14 gives us further insight into the dynamics of these meetings saying, *"Well, my brothers and sisters, let's summarize. When you meet together, one will sing, another will teach, another will tell some special revelation God has given, one will speak in tongues, and another will interpret what is said. But everything that is done must strengthen all of you."(1 Cor 14:26)* These verses talk of whole group participation and spontaneity. Paul goes on to say, *"Let two or three people prophesy, and let the others evaluate what is said. But if someone is prophesying and another person receives a revelation from the Lord, the one who is speaking must stop. In this way, all who prophesy will have a turn to speak, one after the other, so that everyone will learn and be encouraged. Remember that people who prophesy are in control of their spirit and can take turns. For God is not a God of disorder but of peace, as in all the meetings of God's holy people." (1 Cor 14:29-33)* If there was a problem in Corinth it was that so many people had something to bring to the group that they were all trying to talk over one another! Paul had to remind them to take turns and do things in an orderly way. This group participation we read about is a far cry from everyone coming to sit passively, face forward, and then going home.

At the *Introduction to Christianity* courses that we do with the international students, we all gather in someone's home and the host prepares a meal. Generally there are around 25-40 people on any given week. We eat together and have a chat, getting to know one another better and developing friendships. Then we have a bit of worship, maybe just with an acoustic guitar or piano. Song sheets are handed out so that everyone knows the words. We then move onto some teaching which lasts for about 20 minutes before breaking into still smaller groups to discuss things. Often these small group discussions centre around the evening's teaching, but just as often the conversations will go 'off-piste' and we end up talking about the real problems and questions that people within the group are currently facing. People can ask any question they want there and the leaders and mature Christians are spread throughout the groups to provide answers and direction. I've often thought this format is actually much closer to true church than the Sunday morning services. This is the kind of picture the Bible very much portrays in Acts.

## THEY ERADICATED POVERTY

Notice also this description of their community:

*"They sold their property and possessions and shared the money with those in need." - Acts2:45*

It was a community that was full of incredible selflessness and generosity. Those who had a lot were willing to sell what they had so they could give the money to those who needed it more. This idea is repeated later on in Acts:

*"All the believers were united in heart and mind. And they felt that what they owned was not their own, so they shared everything they had. The apostles testified powerfully to the resurrection of the Lord Jesus, and God's great blessing was upon them all. There were no needy people among them, because those who owned land or houses would sell them and bring the money to the apostles to give to those in need.*

*For instance, there was Joseph, the one the apostles nicknamed Barnabas (which means "Son of Encouragement"). He was from the tribe of Levi and came from the island of Cyprus. He sold a field he owned and brought the money to the apostles." - Acts 4:32-37*

I find these to be stunning words. In the early Christian community there was **no** poverty amongst them. None. They completely eradicated it. Think about that. Isn't that astonishing? Those who had enough were freely giving to those who didn't. Possessions had become quite meaningless in this community and they didn't attach much importance to wealth. They were living for something much greater, recognised this life is fleeting, and were now simply motivated to helping one another out in practical ways. In a world filled with greed and selfishness, what a testimony that must have been. Outsiders would have looked on and saw this distinct model community freely giving their wealth to one another and thought something very strange but very special was going on amongst them.

Can you imagine what that would look like today? In *Stay Free* I talked a lot about showing love in authentic, spontaneous and extravagant ways, but could we even begin to consider that kind of generosity? Showing love to one another isn't holding hands and saying nice platitudes to one another. It's actually going to people and asking them, "is there anything you need? Is there anything I can help you with?" And then being practical in following through on it.

This raises another important point. Notice how the Christians first took care of their brothers and sisters in Christ before they took care of the rest of the world? That should be our goal too. Yes, give charitably to everyone who needs it, but make sure that your Christian family are provided for as a matter of priority. Plenty of Christians are suffering in the world today, plenty are being persecuted, plenty are in need of a helping hand, and we should be a community who cares for one another. The world should be able to see this love in action and see how different we are.

Indeed, you'll notice throughout the book of Acts that the love of Jesus is spread in ever increasing circles. That's a good model to follow. At the beginning of Acts it comes to a small room in Jerusalem, then it spreads out to the wider city, then to the outlying towns in Judea and Samaria, then into Eastern Europe, and by the end of the book it's gone all the way to Rome. How does that principle apply to us? Well, when you give to charity, make sure your Christian family are taken care of first. Give to Christian enterprises and ministries as a matter of priority rather than secular ones. If you're a business owner and need employees, look to support Christians with the job positions first so that they can afford to eat and pay their bills. The Christian community should be looking out for on another. As Paul wrote, *"Therefore, whenever we have the opportunity, we should do good to everyone—**especially to those in the family of faith.**" (Gal 6:10)(Emphasis added)* Everyone should get our help, but *especially* those in the Christian family.

This in-to-out principle also applies to your literal family. If you're a father who is a pastor or evangelist, make sure your kids are learning about the Word of God before you look to give it to people on the street. Don't neglect the people closest to you but instead start with them. Then work outwards.

### They Evangelised In Public

*"Then Peter stepped forward with the eleven other apostles and shouted to the crowd, "Listen carefully, all of you, fellow Jews and residents of Jerusalem! Make no mistake about this...<Peter preaches the Gospel to the crowds>...Those who believed what*

*Peter said were baptised and added to the church that day - about 3,000 in all."- Acts 2:14-41*

*"And each day the Lord added to their fellowship those who were being saved."- Acts 2:47*

Of course, the believers didn't just meet together; they went out together too. The tidal motion of discipleship was there. Here we see Peter, supported by the other eleven disciples, publicly proclaiming the Gospel to the crowds and at the end of his message the Bible records about 3,000 being saved and baptised. Would 3,000 people have been added that day if Peter had preached the Gospel to the already-converted inside the upper room? Of course not. He went out to the crowds and preached the Gospel to those who hadn't yet heard it. Because they went out like this, new people were being added to the church every single day. And every single day they were living as a city on a hill for all the world to see.

Notice also from these verses that the new believers were baptised and added to the church straight away. No membership courses. No baptismal classes. No sitting down in an office with elders and being cross-examined to gauge your suitability. No booklets to read, questionnaires to fill out or contracts to sign. No dress code requirements or denominational oaths of allegiance. No institutional hoops to jump through. No churchianity. As soon as anyone made a confession of faith they were instantly considered to be part of the church and were submerged under water as a sign that their new birth was complete.

We see this graphically when Philip meets the Ethiopian eunuch. After hearing the Gospel the eunuch immediately wants to be baptised. The Bible records it like this: *"As they rode along, they came to some water, and the eunuch said, "Look! There's some water! Why can't I be baptized?" He ordered the carriage to stop, and they went down into the water, and Philip baptized him." - Acts 8:36-38*

The Ethiopian wanted to be baptised so they found the nearest body of water and they did it immediately. <u>There should be no waiting around for special once-a-month baptism services. No courses to go through beforehand.</u> If someone wants to become a Christian and be baptised, then on the basis of their confession of faith they should find some water and get it done as soon as possible. And as a priesthood of all believers, there is no need to rely on professional clergy or an institution to make it official. We are all empowered to make converts and to baptise in the name of the Father, Son and Holy Spirit.

## They Prayed For Healing & Cast Out Demons

*"Peter and John went to the Temple one afternoon to take part in the three o'clock prayer service. As they approached the Temple, a man lame from birth was being carried in. Each day he was put beside the Temple gate, the one called the Beautiful Gate, so he could beg from the people going into the Temple. When he saw Peter and John about to enter, he asked them for some money.*

*Peter and John looked at him intently, and Peter said, "Look at us!" The lame man looked at them eagerly, expecting some money. But Peter said, "I don't have any silver or gold for you. But I'll give you what I have. In the name of Jesus Christ the Nazarene, get up and walk!"*

*Then Peter took the lame man by the right hand and helped him up. And as he did, the man's feet and ankles were instantly* healed and strengthened. He jumped up, stood on his feet, and began to walk! Then, walking, leaping, and praising God, he went into the Temple with them." - Acts 3:1-11

"Crowds came from the villages around Jerusalem, bringing their sick and those possessed by evil spirits, and they were all healed." - Acts 5:16

Because the early church was living righteously and going out into the community to preach the Gospel, the power of God was with them and signs and wonders followed them wherever they went. This added credibility to their claims about the risen Christ and many people believed on the evidence of the miraculous signs.

Furthermore, the church also cast out demons. Jesus encountered demons frequently in the Gospels and when we get into the book of Acts, we discover that they're still there, tormenting individuals, causing sickness and looking to steal, kill and destroy. Demons didn't stop their activity when Jesus was resurrected and they didn't decide to go on holiday when the last word in the Bible was written down either. The same evil spirits that Jesus and the apostles had to deal with so frequently in the Bible exist today. The church therefore needs to continue to recognise their presence and drive them out by the power of the Spirit in Jesus' name.

But notice Jesus' words at the Great Commission: *"Go into all the world and preach the Good News to everyone. Anyone who believes and is baptized will be saved. But anyone who refuses to believe will be condemned. These miraculous signs will accompany those who believe: They will cast out demons in my name, and they will speak in new languages. They will be able to handle snakes with safety, and if they drink anything poisonous, it won't hurt them. They will be able to place their hands on the sick, and they will be healed."* (Mark 16:15-18) The first word is the most important here. Miraculous signs will accompany us as we **go**.

And remember what James says: *"Are any of you sick? You should call for the elders of the church to come and pray over you, anointing you with oil in the name of the Lord. Such a prayer offered in faith will heal the sick, and the Lord will make you well. And if you have committed any sins, you will be forgiven. Confess your sins to each other and pray for each other so that you may be healed. The earnest prayer of a righteous person has great power and produces wonderful results."(James 5:14-16)* Only the prayers of the righteous have great power and produce results.

## They Continued In Spite of Persecution

*"But Peter and John replied, "Do you think God wants us to obey you rather than him? We cannot stop telling about everything we have seen and heard.""* - Acts 4

In Acts 4 we see that because the early church was confronting evil in their society, it was beginning to suffer persecution. This is a natural consequence and nothing to be surprised about. Jesus told them this would happen. But importantly, they continued in spite of the persecution. It didn't cause them to retreat into a bubble. And the resistance, in fact, made them stronger. It gave them spiritual muscles. The Bible tells us that, *"The apostles left the high council rejoicing that God had counted them worthy to suffer disgrace for the name of Jesus."* (Acts 5:41) They actually considered it an honour to be persecuted for Jesus because it meant they were on the right track. So here's something to remember: If you are not being persecuted for your faith somehow, the likelihood is that you're not living it properly. Don't go looking for persecution by any means but if you're really confronting an evil society with the truth about Christ, persecution is going to come to you eventually. When it comes, don't worry about it. Resistance makes you stronger and you are blessed if you suffer for the sake of righteousness, even if you are disgraced in the eyes of the world.

The early church were, in fact, becoming stronger through the persecution and were developing into experienced veterans in sharing the Gospel. The Spirit of God was with them and their shared experiences bonded them closer together. Indeed there is a strong sense when you read the book of Acts that despite the attacks, the world didn't stand a chance. The early church was an irresistible force.

*""Blessed are you when you are persecuted," says Jesus. Biblical Christianity is a healthy threat to pagan godlessness and sinfulness, a world overcome by greed, materialism, jealousy and any amount of demonic standards of ethics, sex, money and power. Contemporary Christianity in many countries is simply too harmless and polite to be worth persecuting. But as Christians again live out New Testament standards of life and, for example, call sin as sin, the natural reaction of the world will be, as it always has been, conversion or persecution. Instead of nesting comfortably in temporary zones of religious liberty, Christians will have to prepare to be again discovered as the main culprits standing in the way of global humanism, the modern slavery of having to have fun and the outright worship of Self, the wrong centre of the universe. That is why Christians*

*will and must feel the "repressive tolerance" of a world which has lost its absolutes and therefore refuses to recognize and obey its creator God with His absolute standards. Coupled with the growing ideologization, privatization and spiritualization of politics and economics, Christians will - sooner than most think - have their chance to stand happily accused in the company of Jesus. They need to prepare now for the future by developing a persecution-proof spirit and an even more persecution-proof structure." - Wolfgang Simpson*

We've already seen that the persecution-proof structure is the Chinese structure of the Bible rather than the Russian structure. It is small, self-replicating groups, where every individual is empowered and able to lead in some way. That way, when they take the institutions away, the church will remain.

It's also important to notice again that because of the reality of what the early church were facing, their meetings became more authentic. Acts 12:5 tells us that *"while Peter was in prison, the church prayed very earnestly for him."* That word "earnest" is the key word there. Suddenly their prayers were focused, determined, sincere and deep because they were facing real challenges. In these situations their prayers were often the difference between life and death. As we explored earlier, teaching, worship and prayer all becomes more desperate and authentic when we're applying the Word and getting ourselves into situations where we need God to come through for us. And indeed, God did come through for Peter on this occasion, miraculously setting him free from prison (Acts 12:6-19).

That focus and sincerity led them into fasting too. Acts 13:3 records fasting prior to the sending out of Paul and Barnabas.

*"So after more fasting and prayer, the men laid their hands on them and sent them on their way." - Acts 13:3*

## THEY DID PRACTICAL THINGS

*"But as the believers rapidly multiplied, there were rumblings of discontent. The Greek-speaking believers complained about the Hebrew-speaking believers, saying that their widows were being discriminated against in the daily distribution of food.*

*So the Twelve called a meeting of all the believers. They said, "We apostles should spend our time teaching the word of God, not running a food program. And so, brothers, select seven men who are well respected and are full of the Spirit and wisdom. We will give them this responsibility." - Acts 6:2*

Here we see that the church had established a food distribution program so that nobody would go hungry each day - especially not the weakest among them. In other words they did practical things.

Also notice also that the food program was primarily designed to meet the needs of fellow Christians. They looked after their own family first. But that's not to say their love and generosity didn't extend outwards into the larger community. Later on in Acts we read about a woman called Tabitha. It says, "*There was a believer in Joppa named Tabitha (which in Greek is Dorcas). She was always doing kind things for others and helping the poor. (Acts 9:36)*

Christians were generally known for living selfless lives full of free giving and practical help to those who needed it.

James supports the idea saying: *"Suppose you see a brother or sister who has no food or clothing, and you say, "Good-bye and have a good day; stay warm and eat well"—but then you don't give that person any food or clothing. What good does that do?"* (James 2:15-16)

No doubt they would also have followed the wisdom of Solomon when he said, *"Do not withhold good from those who deserve it when it's in your power to help them. If you can help your neighbor now, don't say, "Come back tomorrow, and then I'll help you." (Proverbs 3:27-28)*

The early church was practical and prompt in their expressions of love for others.

Notice also from the passage that responsibility was delegated and other individuals were empowered to lead in their own way.

## THEY DIDN'T BLINDLY FOLLOW TRADITION

*"The next day as Cornelius's messengers were nearing the town, Peter went up on the flat roof to pray. It was about noon, and he was hungry. But while a meal was being prepared, he fell into a trance. He saw the sky open, and something like a large sheet was let down by its four corners. In the sheet were all sorts of animals, reptiles, and birds. Then a voice said to him, "Get up, Peter; kill and eat them."*

*"No, Lord," Peter declared. "I have never eaten anything that our Jewish laws have declared impure and unclean."*

But the voice spoke again: "Do not call something unclean if God has made it clean." The same vision was repeated three times. Then the sheet was suddenly pulled up to heaven.

Peter was very perplexed. What could the vision mean? Just then the men sent by Cornelius found Simon's house. Standing outside the gate, they asked if a man named Simon Peter was staying there.

Meanwhile, as Peter was puzzling over the vision, the Holy Spirit said to him, "Three men have come looking for you. Get up, go downstairs, and go with them without hesitation. Don't worry, for I have sent them."

So Peter went down and said, "I'm the man you are looking for. Why have you come?"

They said, "We were sent by Cornelius, a Roman officer. He is a devout and God-fearing man, well respected by all the Jews. A holy angel instructed him to summon you to his house so that he can hear your message." So Peter invited the men to stay for the night. The next day he went with them, accompanied by some of the brothers from Joppa.

They arrived in Caesarea the following day. Cornelius was waiting for them and had called together his relatives and close friends. As Peter entered his home, Cornelius fell at his feet and worshiped him. But Peter pulled him up and said, "Stand up! I'm a human being just like you!" So they talked together and went inside, where many others were assembled.

Peter told them, "You know it is against our laws for a Jewish man to enter a Gentile home like this or to associate with you.

*But God has shown me that I should no longer think of anyone as impure or unclean. So I came without objection as soon as I was sent for. Now tell me why you sent for me." - Acts 10:9-33*

Deep-seated tradition stated that Jews should not go to Gentile homes or associate with Gentiles in any way. This idea didn't find its root in the Old Testament but was rather a man-made custom. The people of Israel had traditionally been used to thinking of Gentiles as inferior to themselves because they were the chosen people of God while everyone else was just a Godless pagan. Even though Peter had come to know the truth about Christ, he still retained this cultural mindset. So when God sent this vision to tell him to put his prejudices away and to accept all men as equals, he protested fiercely. God had to repeat the vision three times to get Peter to understand this wasn't up for negotiation. Jesus had created a way for all men from all nations to come to the Father God. Peter was obedient to the command, dropped the cultural mindset that would otherwise have prevented him from fulfilling God's plan, and went to see Cornelius. He didn't stubbornly continue to follow the Jewish tradition because it was the way things had always been done. He was humble enough to change track when the truth was revealed to him, and he let the traditions go. That doesn't mean it wasn't a battle. Paul records a confrontation with Peter in Galatians because Peter was still struggling to let go of the mindset (Gal 2:11-16), but let go of it he did. So it must be with us. Unhelpful, outdated, churchy, stale, counter-productive, archaic, man-made traditions, must die on the altar of truth and authenticity.

## THEY TURNED THE WORLD UPSIDE DOWN

*""Paul and Silas have caused trouble all over the world," they shouted, "and now they are here disturbing our city, too." (Acts 17:6)*

This is one of my favourite verses in the Bible. The world should know when Christians are around. Paul and Silas had been causing revivals or riots wherever they had gone and word of what they were doing had spread far and wide. Let it be said of the church today that we have turned the world upside down with that good kind of trouble-making mentioned here in Acts. The kind that confronts evil and glorifies God for all the world to see.

## Conclusion

Does the picture of the New Testament church in this chapter match the one I've been trying to paint throughout this book? I think it does. What we're looking at in the New Testament is a church that is very different from the one we have come to know. We're looking at a church that was willing to shed traditions and live authentically; a church that formed an informal community and promoted a whole new way of living; a church that was visible and distinct within the larger society; a church that met together, prayed together, worshipped together, taught together and then went out to change the world together; a church that took the commands of Jesus literally; a church that was productive; a church with integrity that was practicing what it preached.

Our task now is simply to get back to that. To shed our insular traditions and hypocritical rituals, our apathy and fear, so that we can start really knowing God and making him known.

# Chapter 14

# We Need Words And Deeds

*"Those who teach by their doctrine must teach by their life, or else they pull down with one hand what they build up with the other." - Matthew Henry*

---

Are we ready to get into small groups and go change the world now?

When Jesus talked about his mission on earth he made it pretty clear: *"The Son of Man came to seek and save those who are lost."* (Luke 19:10) He made it equally clear about passing that responsibility onto his disciples too. And he said we were to do it in two ways - by our words and our deeds.

In the Great Commission he told us *"Go into all the world and **preach** the Good News to everyone."* Words.

He also told us, *"You are the light of the world—like a city on a hilltop that cannot be hidden. No one lights a lamp and then puts it under a basket. Instead, a lamp is placed on a stand, where it gives light to everyone in the house. In the same way, let your good **deeds** shine out for all to see, so that everyone will praise your heavenly Father."* (Matt 5:14-16) Deeds.

Jesus himself was our example in this. He both spoke the truth and he acted powerfully. And then he said, *"Disciples are not greater than their teacher. But the disciple who is fully trained will become like their teacher."* (Luke 6:40) The whole point of being a disciple of Jesus is to become like Him and to emulate him and to carry on his ministry. To say what he said and to do what he did.

Words and deeds. Both are equally important.

If we are all words and no deeds, we are hypocrites. There's no point telling people about Jesus' love and the Kingdom of God if we're not demonstrating it. On the other hand, if we're all deeds and no words, getting involved in social justice and activism, but never telling people how to find salvation in Christ, we're basically only making their journey to hell more pleasurable.

Therefore, if you are vocal about your faith and are sharing it with others regularly, now think about how you can be an activist and do good to your neighbours in practical ways. On the other hand, if you are full of activism but never tell anyone that it's faith in Jesus that is fuelling your actions and that he is the only way to everlasting life, it's time to start letting the world know about that as you go. Christianity is about words and actions combining in perfect harmony, by a people of integrity, living to emulate their Saviour. We need to speak about him and demonstrate his love in equal measure.

## WORDS

How do we reach people with our words?

It can be a daunting thought. A lot of people are scared to share the Gospel because of the backlash and the social stigma. That's something we just have to push through. When Jesus said, *"Everyone who acknowledges me publicly here on earth, I will also acknowledge before my Father in heaven. But everyone who denies me here on earth, I will also deny before my Father in heaven" (Matt 10:32-33)* he ended the idea that faith in him could be a private endeavour. We must proclaim the truth for all the world to hear. Working in groups helps here because we can support and strengthen one another as we go. But persecution will occur and that's something we have to face up to.

Some people are also scared because they don't think they'll know how to answer the myriad of questions that will inevitably be thrown at them. Questions about dinosaurs; Evolution; The historical accuracy of the Bible; Apocryphal Gospels; Why babies die; How a good God can send people to hell; The crusades; A show this guy saw last night that claimed Jesus never existed; Noah's Ark; Who the Nephilim were; Geological questions; Historical questions; Cosmological questions; Why the Bible said not to weave from two types of material. It can sometimes feel like Christians have to be a walking encyclopaedia to witness effectively and often we lose heart before we even begin.

The group dynamic comes in useful again here - many brains are better than one - but the truth is, no matter how much you know, there will always be new questions or theories you haven't heard before and can't answer. Indeed, it's been said that one fool can ask more questions than ten wise men can ever hope to answer. And it's true. But does that mean we should give up? And do we really have to become professors in multiple subjects before we even begin to tell people about Jesus?

The short answer is, no.

While we must make every effort to learn as much as we can, there is a secret that quickly becomes apparent when evangelising - intellectual objections to God are more often than not, just a smokescreen. In other words, while atheists claim that they can't believe in God for purely intellectual and scientific reasons, it's very rarely the case. The truth is that atheists primarily don't *want* to believe in God, and so they deliberately try to build intellectual scaffolding or defences around what they have already decided they would *like* to be true. Why don't atheists want God to exist? Because if God exists they have to bow the knee to him. They're not in control of their own lives anymore. Their own selfish permissive rules don't matter; God's moral law overrides them all. Suddenly they are responsible to Him for their sin and are faced with terrifying judgement. In other words, an atheist can't find God for the same reason a criminal can't find a police officer. Atheists don't want to face up to judgement. They want to remain self-centred and at liberty to follow the Satanic creed - "do what thou wilt".

The problem for them is that a part of them already knows God exists. This is partly because he has made it obvious to them through creation (Romans 1:18-23) and partly because he has written his law in their hearts. The Bible says, *"They demonstrate that God's law is written in their hearts, for their own conscience and thoughts either accuse them or tell them they are doing right." (Rom 2:15)* Because God has written his law on every human heart, atheists find that their own conscience testifies about God and accuses them of their sin from within. This is a severe agitation for them. Therefore, they want very badly for God to go away so that hopefully the guilt they feel will go away too. To this end they rage in vain against a God that they claim not to believe in and look for anyone or anything to support what they have already decided to believe.

What they are experiencing is something known as *cognitive dissonance*. It just means an inner discomfort which occurs when people simultaneously hold two conflicting beliefs. Atheists don't want to believe in God but simultaneously can't help but believe in God because the truth is written on their heart. And this state of dissonance leads to inner frustration, anger, guilt, anxiety and dread. That's why you get these militant atheists who seem to talk more about God than those who actually worship him. Thomas Nagel said, *"I want atheism to be true and am made uneasy by the fact that some of the most intelligent and well-informed people I know are religious believers. It isn't just that I don't believe in God and, naturally, I hope that I'm right in my belief. It's that I hope there's no God! I don't want there to be a God; I don't want the universe to be like that."* These atheists will only ever find peace for their soul when they admit the truth that God is God but in the meantime, they try to bring inner equilibrium and peace by actively looking for intellectual ideas that support what they would like to be true.

At the heart of it all then is rebellion against God; not science or logic.

When you talk to someone about Jesus then, you're often not really looking to reach their intellect. All these smokescreen objections about dinosaurs and rock formations are mainly just distractions from the root of the issue. Instead you often need to bypass the intellect and go to the heart - that place where God's laws are already written - and the truth of what your saying will resonate and bring conviction of sin. All because the law of God already exists within them and bears witness to what you're saying.

This is all very abstract but let me make it real and give you a template with which you can witness to anyone - from professors to builders to brain surgeons or street cleaners.

## Law Then Grace

The key to the whole thing is to offer law first, then grace. Why?

Well, imagine if you went to a random guy with a hypodermic needle and said, "I've got some great news for you! A scientist has discovered a cure for cancer and here it is! Just inject it now and your cancer will be cured!" The guy would be confused, suspicious and possibly even a little offended. He'd say, "Wait, I don't even have cancer. You've got the wrong person!" However, if you said, "Hey, you know that test you went for last week? It showed up cancer. Look, here are the results. But don't worry, I've got some great news for you! A scientist has discovered the cure for cancer and here it is! Just inject it now and your cancer will be cured." This time the guy won't be offended. In fact, he'll crave the cure you're offering him. What you needed to do was show him the proof that he was ill before he was willing to accept the cure. When he understands the nature of his illness, the cure is no longer confusing, pointless or offensive. Suddenly the cure is his pathway to life and he's grateful for it.

Similarly, if you go up to people on the street and tell them the good news that Jesus has died for their sins, it sounds foolish and offensive. The Bible actually says, *"The message of the cross is foolish to those who are headed for destruction!" (1 Cor 1:18)* Why does it sound like foolishness? Because they don't understand what they've done wrong. They don't understand their illness. Their mind has been darkened and they are walking around thinking they're a pretty good kind of person and if there's a heaven, they'll definitely be going. They don't understand that all have sinned and all fall short of God's glorious standard. So to insinuate they're going to hell or that they need a Saviour is offensive to them. As far as they're concerned, God couldn't possibly turn them away.

The first thing Christians have to do then, is to make sure that people are fully aware that they have sinned by breaking God's law.

Romans 3:19-20 says, *"Obviously, the law applies to those to whom it was given, for its purpose is to keep people from having excuses, and to show that the entire world is guilty before God. For no one can ever be made right with God by doing what the law commands. The law simply shows us how sinful we are."*

*"...it was the law that showed me my sin. I would never have known that coveting is wrong if the law had not said, "You must not covet." (Romans 7:7)*

So the purpose of the law is to show us our sin. To show us our disease. To show us our debt. It shows us that we are helpless and guilty before a Holy God. It is the bad news that we need to deliver in order for the subsequent good news to make sense. This is why the law must precede the grace of the good news.

## A Simple Method

So here's a simple method for delivering the Gospel to anyone. You don't need to be a walking encyclopaedia. Just show them how they have broken God's law.

Ask them if they've ever lied.

Ask them if they've ever stolen.

Ask them if they've ever taken the name of God in vain.

Ask them if they've ever looked at someone with lust.

Ask them if they've ever hated anyone.

If the person is being honest, they'll answer 'yes' to each of these questions. This means they're a liar, thief, blasphemer and according to the Bible, an adulterer and murderer at heart. (Matt 5:28 & 1 John 3:15)

Ask the person to consider whether they would be found innocent or guilty if they were to be judged by these crimes. If honest, they'll admit they're guilty.

Ask them if they're guilty, will they go to heaven or hell. Do liars, thieves and blasphemers really merit heaven? If they're honest, they'll admit that heaven isn't their natural destination after all. They'll admit that justice demands punishment.

Remind them that the Bible says, *"for all have sinned; we all fall short of God's glorious standard." (Rom 3:23)* and that the wages of sin are death (Rom 6:23).

This lets them know that we're all in the same boat. We've *all* sinned and therefore the natural destination of every single human being is hell. The law has left us all helpless and without excuse before God.

The heart has now been prepared for the Good News. They're now aware of their disease and ready for the cure. They're now aware of their debt and ready to hear about the one who paid the price. Now you're ready to tell them about how Jesus died on the cross to take the punishment for the sin that we deserved upon his shoulders so that we can have everlasting life.

Law then Grace. It's a simple system. It bypasses the intellect and goes straight to the heart, which is where it matters.

Beware though. As soon as you hit that tender spot in their conscience and remind them of the sin they don't want to see, their cognitive dissonance may go into overdrive and there may well be a backlash of defensiveness. Fury, frustration, guilt, anxiety and dread will bubble up inside them and might come spilling out through venomous words. As the one who is stirring those feelings, you may well be on the receiving end. Just remember to keep speaking *in love* and make sure they hear the Good News of the Gospel before you leave. Anger is actually better than apathy as it shows their conscience is at least still sharp enough to make them feel uncomfortable.

Finally, while you don't have to be a walking encyclopaedia, it does help a lot if you can show you've put some thought into the tough questions. Do some reading on the arguments against the faith. Learn apologetics. Learn about science. Learn about history. The answers are all there, the truth can stand up to the scrutiny. We should be training ourselves to know it, proclaim it and defend it. The method above is only a template so you always have something to fall back on. You don't need to follow it exactly. Just make some kind of effort. Something is always better than nothing. In fact, check out this link for the story of a man who didn't go through the law then grace method but who just made sure he did something every single day of his life, and who had a massive impact on the people he met: http://www.youtube.com/watch?v=h76MHjjGu08. The Holy Spirit can use anyone.

## Deeds

As well as words, we need deeds.

The things we do to make an impact on the world can be so wide-ranging that it's a whole other series in itself, and indeed, one day it will be. The next phase of the Fuel Project is to produce a series of videos under the name "Kindling." Like the name suggests, these Kindling videos will be designed to ignite Christian activism in our local communities through New Testament style small groups. Truly we can be extravagant with love in countless innovative, fun and practical ways. The Kindling series will aim to inspire the church in those things.

However, if you don't want to wait around for the Kindling series and would like to get a group together and do something straight away, here are just a few ideas to get you started. Some of these sound completely frivolous but the idea is just to start promoting habit-forming, selfless living. To this end, even the tiniest acts of kindness can help. But go as big as you want on these. And remember to always accompany them with the proclamation of the Gospel in some way. People must know what is motivating you and Jesus must get the credit. You can do this in spoken or in written form. That is, you can either tell people about the Jesus verbally or simply leave gospel tracts as you go:

- Raise funds for charity by doing a sponsored, walk, climb, swim, dance...anything. Think of something fun. You could also ask the local press to cover it.

- Skip a meal and give the money to charity or take the food to a food bank.

- Have a clear out and take things to the charity shop.

- Give up your place in a queue. Maybe even pay for the shopping of the person behind you if you're at the supermarket.

- Do chores or run errands for people in your neighbourhood. E.g. Offer to wash their car or cut their grass. Do it as a group.

- Do a neighbourhood clean-up. Wear something that lets people know you're a Christian group so that passing cars and pedestrians see what's going on. Be prepared to witness to anyone who stops to chat.

- Do the "Tract Drop Game" where you each compete to leave tracts in the most innovative and daring places. For example, inside copies of the "Origin of Species" or "the God Delusion" in bookstores, left with tips at restaurants, inside wallets in department stores etc. Take photos each time you do this. This is a fun way of getting the Gospel out.

- Bake things and then take them out to the community. Give them away free of charge.

- Have a 'no TV evening' and play board games instead. Either with family or your group.

- Find BOGOF vouchers. Give the free one away.

- Live on £1.40 a day. A lot of people in the world live on only this amount. Put yourself in their shoes then pray about it and consider giving money to help these people.

- Walk around the neighbourhood together and pray about what you see. Whether it be good things or bad things. If you can practically do something about the problems you see, then work out a plan to meet the needs.

- Go through the newspaper and pray about articles you see. Again, look for ways to help practically with any local issues.

- Savour experiences together. In other words, learn thankfulness. Go for a hike, play sports together. Enjoy your group's company.

- Give a home made gift to someone.

- Babysit for friends.

- Give blood.

- Plant flowers somewhere to be seen. Or trees.

- Do street evangelism. If you want to have a go at street preaching, go for it. Or you can do public drama skits and tell stories which drive home Godly truths.

- Preach the word on social networking sites.

- Find local or national Christian causes to support. Email MPs and sign petitions about issues affecting Christianity. Campaign and go on marches. Make the Christian voice heard.

- Have a Bible study and whenever you read about an activity of the church, make a plan to emulate it.

- Volunteer.

- Repaint walls tarnished by graffiti.

- Create a flashmob idea with a Christian message and perform it in a public place.

You get the idea. Just demonstrate love with your good deeds and make sure Jesus gets the glory and people get the Gospel. Be consistent about this. Don't just do it once for the novelty and then forget. This must become a lifestyle. We must become followers of *The Way*. Get excited about this too. There's a lot of fun to be had in getting your group together and doing worthwhile things in your community. You'll feel amazing afterwards too. That sense of being able to put your head on your pillow at night knowing you made an impact in the world and helped people out can get addictive. As Martin Luther King Jr. said, *"Everybody can be great...because anybody can serve. You don't have to have a college degree to serve. You don't have to make your subject and verb agree to serve. You only need a heart full of grace. A soul generated by love."* - Martin Luther King, Jr

This has just been a cursory glance at the ways we can reach people with words and deeds but we'll be expanding on ideas in the forthcoming Kindling series. In the meantime, have a brainstorming session with your group and come up with creative ideas. In doing so, encourage individuals to flourish with their gifts.

## A Request From The Fuel Project

Now here's an extra special request from the Fuel Project: as you go about these things, if possible, have someone film it. If you don't have access to a video camera, even mobile phones produce HD quality footage these days so you can use those. And even if you still can't get video, take some pictures. Once you have your photographs or video footage, please send them to the Fuel Project. Why?

Well, earlier on I spoke about the need to be visible. We need to be visible to melt cynicism in non-believers but we also need to be visible to inspire fellow-believers to follow our example. As we've explored in this book, believers are scared to step outside of the four walls and to go public with their faith. They're bored and restless but they're too scared to take the risky leap into New Testament Christianity. Others are so locked into a traditional mindset that they don't know what true discipleship and New Testament Christianity actually looks like. I want them to look at what you're doing - you who are putting your faith into action and think, *"hey, we could do that! We could get a group together. That doesn't look so hard. That actually looks kind of inspiring. That actually looks kind of compelling. That actually looks like the church I read about in the Bible!"* And then I want them to follow your lead. We must visibly demonstrate what it looks like to be a true Christian.

The idea is that The Fuel Project will become a repository for inspiring footage from all over the world. We'll tell the stories of those who are putting their faith into action - the living, breathing, organic church - and make it visible to as many people as possible. These stories will either be delivered through the Kindling series or as standalone reports. I want the church to see the things you're doing and be inspired to follow your example in their own communities. So that they'll inspire others. So that they will inspire others etc. We need to create a self-replicating, persecution-proof system of small groups who are truly discipling and who begin to sweep the world like the tornado of 2000 years ago. Because of the increasingly large following we have at The Fuel Project, we now have an opportunity to give this a shot. But it won't work unless we, the church, shake off the chains of apathy and fear that hold us down and rouse ourselves into action. It will require us to embrace a life of risk-taking, adventurous faith.

As we move into this new phase for the Fuel Project I plan to make it a significant part of the ministry to visit places where the church is putting faith into action to make these Kindling reports. If you would like myself and/or a Fuel Project team to come to where you live to record your group in action, whatever it is you're doing, no matter how big or small, then please email authenticfuel@gmail.com to make arrangements. We'll simply capture the work on video and do some interviews so you can explain what's going on. The church needs to see these inspiring stories so that it will be encouraged and won't get tired and give up. Whether you're an official charity, an informal community or even just a few people trying to make a difference, I'll be delighted to tell the story of what God is doing and to make it visible for the world to see.

If you would like to be involved in a Kindling group but don't know anyone locally that you can join up with, you can submit your name to The Fuel Project at authenticfuel@gmail.com. If other people from your area register, we'll put you in touch with one other so you can meet up and get going.

On a technical level, if you plan to record your own footage and have the means to edit it then please do. Otherwise, you can send the unedited footage and we'll work with it here. Please use the highest quality footage you can. Again, authenticfuel@gmail.com is the email address to use if you'd like details of how and where to send the file.

To help you with your evangelism efforts, I'm also looking to start offering tracts through www.thefuelproject.org that you can hand out or leave around. Check out the website when you get a chance. Tracts are often disparaged but they actually have many good benefits. They are economical, they work even when we're sleeping, they have the ability to get to places we can't, they're never afraid, they're never tempted to compromise, they never get tired or discouraged, they stick to their message and never argue and they speak to people when they're in the mood to listen! I'm going to do what we can to get those to you.

Any donations to help with this next phase of the ministry can be made via PayPal to authenticfuel@gmail.com.

At the end of the day, the world can argue with us on theology, intelligent design, the exclusivity of Christ, moral absolutes and any number of other things but what the world can't argue with is a church that is visibly pouring itself out in love for others. That's what really melts hearts and kills cynicism. And that's what inspires other Christians. If you will find the bravery to pioneer the movement, others will find the courage to follow. Like the apostles, you can be part of something that changes the world. Can it be done? We won't know until we try. Is it worth trying to do? Absolutely. There is nothing better than to spend your life in a worthy cause. As Theodore Roosevelt famously said, *"it is not the critic who counts, not the man who points out how the strong man stumbled or where the doer of deeds could have done better. The credit belongs to the man who is actually in the arena; whose face is marred by the dust and sweat and blood; who strives valiantly; who errs and comes short again and again; who knows the great enthusiasms, the great devotions and who spends himself in a worthy cause; who at best knows in the end the triumph of high achievement and who, at worst, if he fails, at least fails while daring greatly, so that his place will never be with those cold and timid souls who know neither victory or defeat."* Do something. Do something. Do something. There's no more worthy cause than the Kingdom of God. And I can pretty much guarantee that once you do this, with all its highs and lows, pains and triumphs, you'll never want to go back to dry, ritualistic, institutional, churchianity.

# Chapter 15

# The Challenge

Earlier on this book I said that true change rarely comes from the top. Normally always it's down to radical small groups of believers with clarity of vision who are not encumbered with the power, wealth or status of the current system. However, I'd like to challenge pastors to reform from within and start truly discipling.

If this book has made sense to you then move away from the idea of church as just a sermon delivered by one guy while the rest sit passively and then go home. Teaching is a powerful tool but you must then empower and mobilise the church so that they will put the points you're making into action. Tear up the template. Appoint leaders to disciple small groups with the aim that they will become leaders of their own one day. Don't let those small groups become endless studies. Instead, emphasise that everyone should apply what they've learned. Don't look primarily to create a place of comfort which people never want to leave; look to create a training camp from which the church goes out. Engage with the community. Encourage mobilisation. Encourage interactivity and participation. Allow questions and discussion so that people get the answers they need. Talk about the things that are affecting people today. Equip the church to evangelise. Equip them to tackle the corrupt culture in which we live. Move away from formal, performance-oriented services and move towards something more informal and authentic. Dispense with idolatrous traditions and empty rituals. Get real, spontaneous, Holy Spirit led, courageous and extravagant with love. Demand righteousness. That's right, demand it. Confront immorality in the church and if there is no repentance, don't be afraid to remove the person from your fellowship (1 Cor 5:2). Only let them back in if they repent. Challenge your men and give them responsibility. Set them difficult goals and then let them do what they were born to do. Put them to work. And let them be innovators, warriors, leaders and adventurers in the process. Preach the Gospel to unbelievers. Go.

If you don't want to change things drastically overnight then keep the Sunday service but at least reform your house group network. Most house groups will meet in an evening during the week and spend the time studying and discussing. Insist that those groups start using the time to plan local action and then actually go out to implement it. Don't try to control the individual house groups as part of a top-down hierarchical structure. Just continually disseminate authority to the house group leaders and let them do what needs to be done. Emphasise that their aim is not just to make converts but to make disciples who can make disciples. The house groups should multiply at least every few years as new leaders emerge from the system.

And now to address the church itself. If you're a Christian and this book has made sense, then please put it in front of your pastor and encourage him to return to a New Testament model. However, if he is unwilling to give up the status quo and you simply cannot find this kind of gathering where you live, and if you're becoming bored with the same old routine, then remember that church is not an institution or building. *You* are the church. So you are free to get some friends together and organically create a small group of your own to put these principles into action. Be China rather than Russia. Congregate in homes and be proactive. Form a group of no more than thirty people. There's no need to be legalistic about that but research shows that once a group grows beyond even twelve people, some of the group will back away from full participation and the more dominant members will start to view the rest as an audience. We want to make sure that this doesn't happen and we want to keep everyone engaged, valued and participating with their unique gifts. If some people are starting to get sidelined as the group gets too big, it's time to divide into two to allow for more growth. A useful image is to think of is a cell. A cell multiplies by continually dividing itself in two. Do that.

Create an informal family type atmosphere. When you meet in the evenings for example, don't have dinner beforehand but incorporate it into the gathering. Eat together, pray together and plan together. Create an environment of trust, confidentiality and honesty with one another, provide for each other's needs, and strengthen one another for the work ahead. Set goals in your community. It can be anything. And then go make it happen. Support one another when persecution comes. Because if you're doing it right, it certainly will.

Like I have already mentioned, I believe God is telling us to adopt this model because it won't be long before the church is stripped of its buildings and all the institutional props that we currently rely on won't be there for much longer anyway. The time of the Anti-Christ is fast approaching and this Biblical model will allow us to survive and thrive in the face of persecution. In fact, just as the New Testament church thrived in the face of persecution in the 1st Century, the Chinese church which has adopted the same model thrives in the face of persecution today. If the employment of this method has historically always coincided with incredible church growth and revival, perhaps we should learn from history? By not adhering to this model and sticking with the Russian form, we're leaving ourselves open to decimation when the Anti-Christ comes and the tribulation begins. In other words, the small group format represent the best hope for church renewal in our times and it represents our best hope for times of oppression in the future. We must prepare in advance.

Yes, this all seems quite radical right now. But historically, all of the New Testament churches looked like this. It only seems radical to us because we've been conditioned by our culture to think of church according to tradition. And the tradition just isn't working. Let's take our cue from the Bible instead. I don't think we'll ever regret it.

The aim of the Fuel Project is to see a network of these small groups emerge around the world. Whether they grow out of established churches or whether they form organically, we just want to see groups of people who are willing to live out their faith in faithful obedience and to be visible about it so that the world will see us and be inspired to praise God in heaven. As we move into the Kindling phase, start getting your group together in anticipation and make something happen wherever you live right now. Use some of the ideas listed earlier and again, you'll hopefully find tracts at www.thefuelproject.org in due course. We'll work on providing further materials in the meantime and remember to either send your footage or invite us over if you prefer.

Again, general correspondence or questions can be sent to authenticfuel@gmail.com. You can find The Fuel Project on Facebook (facebook.com/thefuelproject) or YouTube (YouTube.com/thefuelproject). And as always, if you'd like to contribute to the goals of this ministry, you can donate via PayPal to authenticfuel@gmail.com.

Finally, keep an eye on www.thefuelproject.org for updates and the latest news. A refreshed website should be on the way shortly.

Get excited and may God bless us as we go.

*"Knowing that we are fulfilling God's purpose is the only thing that really gives rest to the restless human heart." - Chuck Colson*

*"There is no peace in the borderlands. The halfway Christian is a torment to himself and of no benefit to others." - Earnest Worker*

Printed in Great Britain
by Amazon.co.uk, Ltd.,
Marston Gate.